BEAUTIFUL STREAM

Beautiful Stream

DISTURBANCE AND RENEWAL ON THE LITTLE NORTH SANTIAM

James P. Quiring

Oregon State University Press Corvallis

Cataloging-in-Publication data is available at the Library of Congress.

LCCN 2026035303

ISBN 978-1-962645-62-1 paper; ISBN 978-1-962645-63-8 ebook

♾ This paper meets the requirements of ANSI/NISO Z39.48-1992 (Permanence of Paper).

First published in 2026 by Oregon State University Press
Printed in the United States of America

Oregon State University
OSU Press

Oregon State University Press
121 The Valley Library
Corvallis OR 97331-4501
541-737-3166 • fax 541-737-3170
www.osupress.oregonstate.edu

Oregon State University Press in Corvallis, Oregon, is located within the traditional homelands of the Marys River or Ampinefu Band of Kalapuya. Following the Willamette Valley Treaty of 1855, Kalapuya people were forcibly removed to reservations in Western Oregon. Today, living descendants of these people are a part of the Confederated Tribes of Grand Ronde Community of Oregon (grandronde.org) and the Confederated Tribes of Siletz Indians (ctsi.nsn.us).

Dedicated to my parents
Jack and Almeda Quiring
for introducing me to the North Fork
and encouraging me to explore

Contents

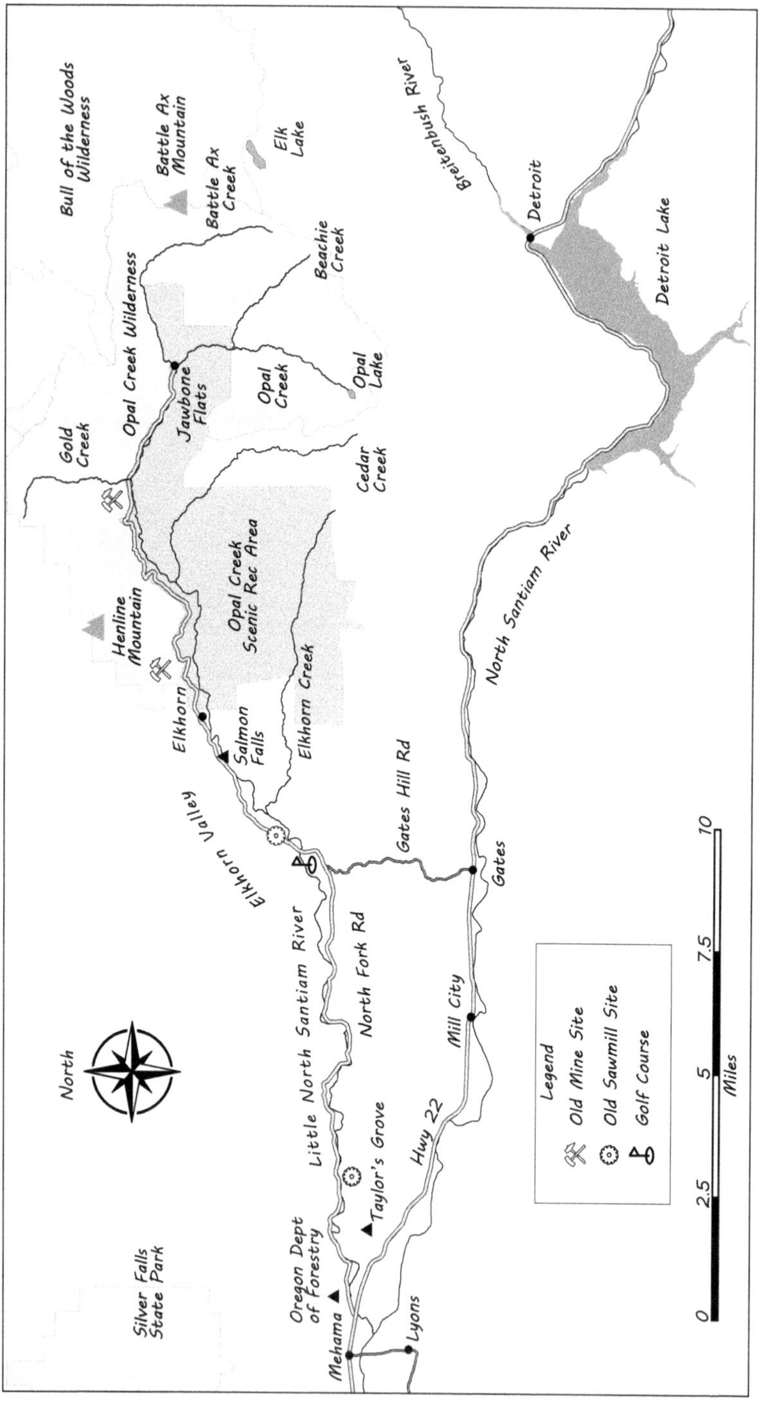

Little North Santiam River (North Fork) map. (*Illustrated by Andy Adkins.*)

The Little North Santiam River

Shining waters flow in every corner of Oregon, and some are widely known: the Columbia, the Willamette, the Rogue, and the Snake, to name a few. But if you quizzed Oregonians about the Little North Santiam River, many might pause for a moment in an effort to recall where it is and then say, "Tell me about it." So, I will.

The Little North Santiam, known to locals as the "North Fork," originates from icy springs in a mountain-rimmed canyon of the Willamette National Forest in western Oregon's Cascade mountains. Its waters first collect on the slopes of an ancient volcano—Battle Ax mountain—at 5,523 feet above sea level in the Opal Creek Wilderness. As these waters come together, they form Battle Ax Creek, which courses downslope through a rock-strewn canyon. Four miles to the west, Opal Creek gathers water in Opal Lake before it tumbles through the wilderness, accepting water from Beachie Creek and then joining with Battle Ax Creek. Here, Opal Creek and Battle Ax Creek combine to form the North Fork.

The North Fork cascades down through the canyon of the Opal Creek Scenic Recreation Area, sometimes squeezed between steep walls that force its flow through slender passageways. Along the way, other streams join the parade, including Gold, Cedar, and Henline Creeks.

Midway through its 27-mile journey, the river widens through the broad and nearly flat Elkhorn Valley and the small community of Elkhorn, where it is joined by the rushing water of Elkhorn Creek. Finally, it completes its westward course through the rugged lower canyon, joined by numerous smaller streams to a point near the small town of Mehama. In this short distance, the river has dropped nearly a vertical mile—and, at 600 feet elevation, the North Fork releases the entirety of the canyon's crystalline water into the mainstem North Santiam River. All of the mountainsides and canyons contributing water to the North Fork form the watershed of the river.

From Mehama, the North Santiam River delivers the North Fork's water west through small farms and rural communities, soon joining the main Santiam River (that collects water from both the North and South Santiam Rivers) and continues west to the Willamette River near Oregon's capital city of Salem. The Willamette drifts gently northward through farmlands of the expansive Willamette Valley, whose rich soils were deposited by deep ancient floods. It then pours over the thunderous Willamette Falls near Portland and eventually into the Columbia River that flows west and empties into the Pacific Ocean.

Wild spring Chinook salmon and wild winter steelhead still navigate the route between the North Fork and the Pacific Ocean—a distance of nearly 200 miles. In spite of water diversions that have been built near Stayton and at Willamette Falls, the linkage of rivers continues to be a prime waterway for these species, as it has been for thousands of years.

For countless centuries, evergreen forests have draped the lands within the North Fork canyon, dominated by Douglas-fir and western hemlock. Towering western redcedar have favored low-lying areas where soils are moist and fertile. Where trees have escaped repeated forest fires over time, these striking giants have reached five hundred to eight hundred or even a thousand years old. Bigleaf maple and red alder have long accented the forest, finding habitat along the banks of the river and its tributaries.

Volcanic cliffs and pinnacles rise like great sculptures and monuments along the canyon's high ridges and surrounding mountain tops. Winters typically bring abundant rain to the lower canyon and deep snow to higher mountains that often lingers into June on shaded north-facing slopes. By contrast, summers are so warm and dry that the trees and plants of the forest have evolved over millennia to become summer-drought-tolerant, surviving with little or no rain from late June to October.

People have come to this river, its mountains, and its canyon since a time deep in human history to gather its resources and, in recent years, to make the canyon their home. Stories about their time here alternately captivate and teach us.

My own family first started coming here when I was very young—more than seventy years ago. Within this book, I have interwoven some

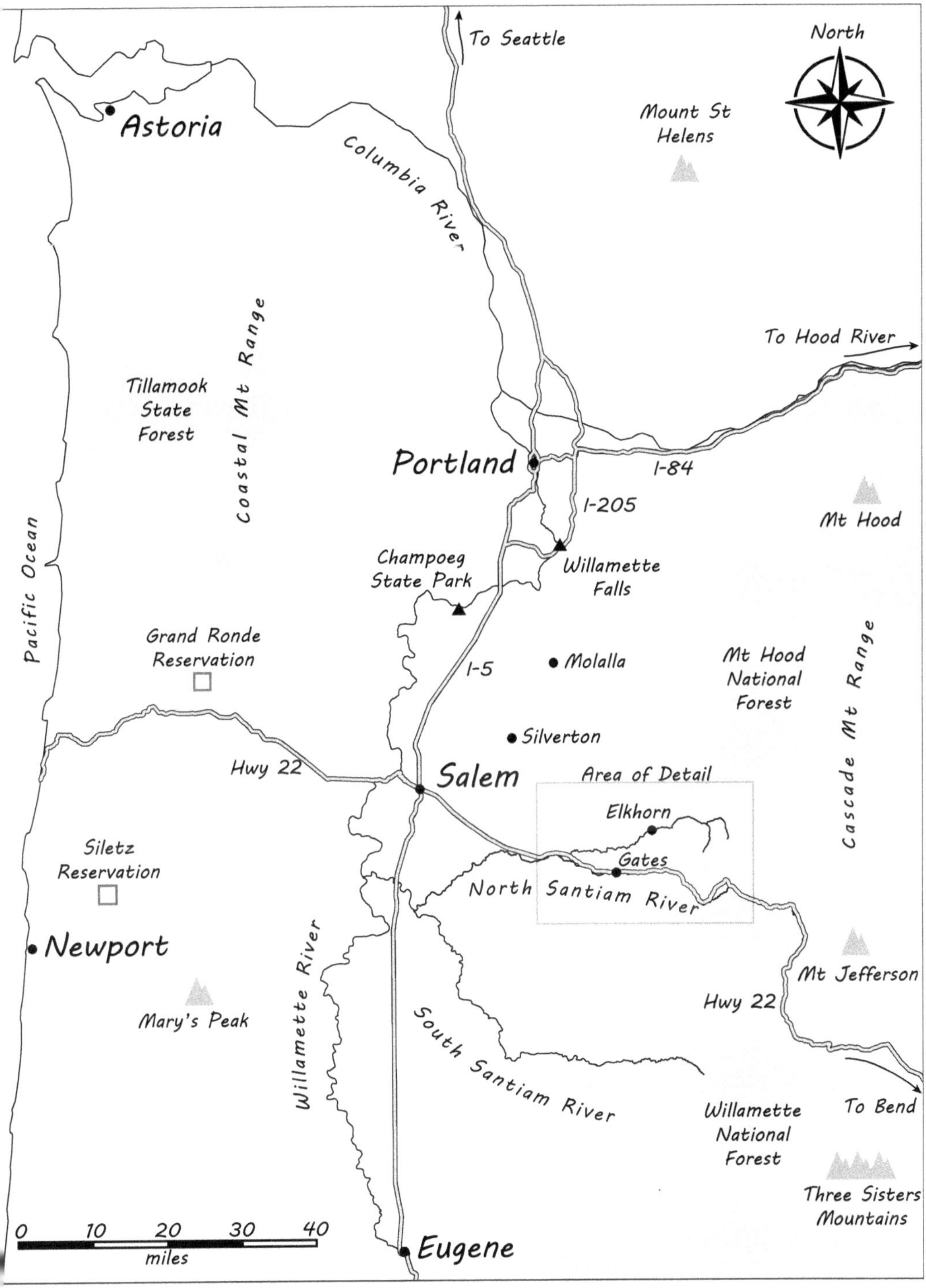

Northwest Oregon map. See inset map on p. viii. (*Illustrated by Andy Adkins.*)

of my personal North Fork experiences with the canyon's deeper history that I have learned only recently. These connections and stories from my life form a backdrop for the history described in the book.

Officially this river is called the Little North Santiam River, although many historic maps and documents refer to it as "The Little North Fork of the Santiam." Most locals call it the Little North Fork or, simply, the North Fork, which is the name my family has used for seventy years and what I call it throughout the book.

Prologue: A Hurricane of Fire

SUNDAY, AUGUST 16, 2020

I was sitting at my writing table on the front deck of our family's Elkhorn cabin on this warm, dry late summer morning, closing in on what I thought to be the final chapter of my manuscript for this book. It was a little after 10 a.m. when I heard a familiar rumbling up the canyon and in the mountains around us.

I called to my partner Shawn through the screen door.

"Did you hear that?"

She had. She leapt onto the deck to listen.

It was an ominous sound, echoing between the steep canyon walls above us. With extreme fire danger, it was not a good day for a thunderstorm.

As we feared, lightning had struck in the mountains to the east. When the storm passed, a small column of smoke began lifting from the forest just 8 miles from the cabin. Staff at the remote Opal Creek Ancient Forest Center at Jawbone Flats smelled the smoke right away and called it in. By 11:30, personnel at a US Forest Service lookout 15 miles south spotted a column rising from a steep mountainside and pinned its location to just above Beachie Creek, a small creek in the upper North Fork canyon.

Forest Service managers quickly committed to fully suppressing it—but fighting even this small blaze would be a challenge. Access in the rugged terrain would be difficult, and a hundred years of aggressive fire suppression had resulted in a large buildup of burnable material throughout area forests. Western Oregon was in drought, and the forest was extremely dry. In addition, the demands of many other fires throughout the western states might limit the availability of fire personnel and equipment.

Within two hours of the fire start, smoke jumpers scouted the area from the air, but the steep and rugged terrain made it impossible to find a place to safely parachute close to the fire. The knife-edge ridges and dense forest made the area virtually impenetrable. Unable to quickly get firefighters on the ground, the Forest Service turned to its next best option: aerial water drops. Using helicopters with water collected from a nearby lake, they doused the fire again and again, limiting its growth to about 10 acres by nightfall.[1]

A team of rappelers arrived the next day with a plan to access the fire by lowering themselves and their gear to the ground by rope from hovering helicopters. But after circling the fire repeatedly, spotters could not find a safe landing site close to the fire; the trees were too tall and the forest too dense.

At the same time, a specially trained "hotshot" firefighting crew pushed toward the fire on foot. After two attempts involving arduous cross-country hikes, they finally reached the fire's edge. What they found were extremely challenging conditions: no reasonable safety zones, lookout points, or helicopter landing sites. In the deep tangle of the forest, they also became aware of threats from falling trees and fire-loosened rocks on the steep slopes that could crash down the mountainside and endanger fire crews. They determined the fire was too hazardous for ground crews and pulled back. For several days, helicopters dropped water until little smoke could be seen. At that point, one chopper was sent back for maintenance and the other was moved to a more rapidly growing fire elsewhere.[2]

Although the fire grew very little during the first few days, my family and I had deep concerns. We feared that even a small blaze in the extremely dry canyon could easily become a much bigger problem, especially if strong winds from the east would arise and push it down canyon toward us. Those with local knowledge of the North Fork know that prevailing winds in late summer and fall can switch from normal moist westerlies off the ocean to strong dry easterlies from the high deserts of Central Oregon. For many years, my family had experienced the canyon's strong east winds and the funneling effect of the narrow canyon just east of our community of some forty homes and cabins. We shared our concerns with neighbors and fire managers.

Thirteen days after the thunderstorm—August 29—my family and I began hearing long-range weather forecasts calling for the possibility of east winds in our area—just the wind direction we had feared. Moreover, as the next few days passed, forecasts indicated that a massive weather

Beachie Creek Fire, September 1, 2020. Officially, the cause of the fire is listed as unknown, while most reports suggest it either started from a lightning strike on August 16 or ignited from a lightning strike several weeks earlier that lay dormant until noticed on August 16. (*US Forest Service photo by Mark Turney.*)

system in Idaho and Montana would bring late-summer snow to the Rocky Mountains, push strong east winds into western Oregon, and create extreme fire weather conditions on the west slope of the Cascade mountains surrounding the North Fork.[3] By Labor Day, the fire had slowly grown to more than 700 acres.

My son-in-law Ben arrived on Labor Day weekend to help fireproof the cabin and property in case flying embers—or the fire itself—should threaten. We removed needles and twigs from the roof and gutters, cut shrubs and small trees close to the cabin, and limbed larger trees. We moved firewood and other flammables away from the cabin.

Through the hot weekend, forecasters issued warnings for critical fire weather. The National Weather Service warned of three days of extreme fire danger starting on Labor Day with humidity as low as 5 percent and conditions that may be favorable for rapid fire spread that may threaten life and property.[4]

The *Statesman Journal* newspaper reported, "An extreme wind event unlike anything Oregon has seen in the history of early September with extremely dry winds of 50 to 75 mph in the forecast." The article quoted a forestry official who compared the forecast to a "hurricane hitting a wildfire."[5]

Eric Johnson, deputy fire staff for Northwest Oregon Fire Management, said, "The fire weather forecasted is extremely rare and occurs only a few times a century."[6]

It was the worst imaginable forecast, and it came as the Beachie Creek Fire continued to creep along. The forest was parched from a hot, dry summer, and the North Fork was a bull's-eye on their forecast map for extreme fire weather.

LABOR DAY—SEPTEMBER 7, 2020

On Labor Day morning, we awoke to a blue windless sky. With temperatures forecast to reach near 90 degrees, we agreed to finish work while the air was still cool. On such a beautiful and calm morning, a rare powerful windstorm was impossible to imagine.

Shawn left for home in Salem in early morning with our stack of cabin journals, my book manuscript, and some personal items. Just before 10 a.m., a text message popped in from a colleague who served as a community liaison for the US Forest Service team in charge of the fire. He alerted us that Elkhorn was being placed on a Level 2 evacuation notice that advised residents to pack belongings and be ready to leave at a moment's notice. Knowing our neighbors would want word as soon as possible, Ben and I immediately activated our neighborhood emergency phone tree. Within minutes, neighbors began alerting others that representatives from the sheriff's office would soon be coming door-to-door to officially announce the notice.

Ben finished outside work as I began gathering family items. I already knew some of the things I wanted to take, beginning with my dad's old fly rod—the one he taught me to fish with when I was a boy. I selected a few cups and dishes—my mom's favorites—hurriedly wrapped them in newspaper, and laid them in the old wooden box with rope handles that dad made many years ago. In addition to gathering a few valuables, I chose things that had special meaning and that connected to our family history. If the fire was to come, at least these irreplaceable items would be saved.

Friends and neighbors called with questions and concerns. Just before noon, I heard a voice through the forest—our neighbor Denise. She hurried over to tell us that county officials had just arrived at her house for a meeting as soon as several neighbors could gather.

The meeting was brief. A search and rescue team confirmed the Level 2 evacuation notice, and further, they advised us to voluntarily leave as soon as possible because it may not be feasible to reach us again if conditions deteriorated rapidly. Understanding the urgency, we hurried back to our cabin to finish packing.

We hauled out my father's hefty writing table—the one that he had made as a young man in the 1920s—and secured it in the truck. I climbed the ladder to the loft and dug out the cabin's original crank telephone from its dusty storage box. I carefully carried it down the ladder and out to my car that was by then nearly packed full. There was still no wind, but we began to smell smoke.

By late afternoon, we put our tools away and tied down the truckload. Ben left the cabin, crossed the river, and headed for home. As he came into view across the river, I rang our old locomotive bell to say farewell. On cue, he honked in reply. This time, saying goodbye to the cabin felt different than any time before.

I locked the shed and went back inside the cabin one last time to close windows and curtains, the way my family had done countless times before when heading home from weekend trips. I drew a slow deep breath and took a long look around at the interior, not wanting to leave. As I stepped outside, a gust of wind hit me, and I saw trees begin to bend. I knew it was time to go.

Barely penetrating the thickening smoke, the eerie sun now appeared as an orange disc surrounded by an aura of deep red. Dry Douglas-fir needles blew from the trees like golden rain. I could not know whether the fire would move down the canyon, but the smoke smelled strong now, and a deeply uneasy feeling filled my stomach.

Mountain views were gone, hidden behind a thickening dome of smoke. I drove out our dirt road as the sun fully disappeared into the deepening pall of gray. It was a little after 5 p.m., and most of our neighbors had already left. I couldn't remember when I had ever experienced the neighborhood so empty and quiet.

Heading down North Fork Road, I slowed to glance at Mrs. Wheeler's old house, which I had visited many times throughout my childhood, then continued down past Salmon Falls. As I pulled over to watch a deer cross the road in Elkhorn Valley, a string of wildland fire trucks passed me in the opposite direction of the fire, an indication that the situation had become critical and unsafe, even for the firefighters.

At the state highway junction, I pulled in next to the Oregon Department of Forestry office and spotted some former colleagues who were working there. I walked over to let them know we had evacuated, and they reported that the best available computer models predicted the fire would likely remain higher in the mountains and not threaten Elkhorn. I told them my experience told me that east winds often funnel down this narrow canyon in a way that might not be picked up by computer models. Huddled together in smoke-filled air, we shared our hopes and concerns—then wished each other well.

I drove my packed car the remaining 25 miles to our home in Salem, which by then had become shrouded in smoke. Shawn had been nervously awaiting my return as she watched our wind vane spin wildly on our front lawn. We turned out the lights at 10 p.m., hoping and praying the morning would bring favorable news.

Just after midnight, my phone started ringing. Caller ID indicated it was an "Emergency Message." Half asleep, we listened to a recorded reverse 911 message announcing that an elevated Level 3 evacuation "Go Now" notice had been issued for the entire 15-mile length of North Fork Road, from our cabin area at Elkhorn all the way to Mehama, as well as extensive areas surrounding the North Fork canyon. We were in shock—this meant the fire must be exploding.

We immediately began thinking of friends in the canyon who may not have gotten word and started making phone calls. Most calls did not go through; connections were already down. We did reach our ninety-two-year-old friend Harriet in Mehama, who drove alone to our Salem house at 2 a.m. after a neighbor had cut and removed a large fallen tree from her driveway and she joined the long slow line of cars headed west away from the fire. She had had time to grab only medications, cell phone, and a framed picture of her late husband.

By morning, the dense black smoke in Salem was accompanied by tiny flecks of falling gray ash. It was hard to grasp that the debris was coming from the forests of the North Fork. After a few hours of restless sleep, we arose to see only a tiny shaft of orange light piercing the smoke from the far northeasterly sky at sunrise; soon even that faded. Although the sun was up, Salem was nearly as dark as midnight. It reminded me of stories about smoke from Oregon's Tillamook Burn and ash from the volcanic eruption of Mount St. Helens that had turned daylight to dark, and I wondered whether this fire would also become part of Oregon history.

Harriet felt certain her house would be gone and began calling family members. To escape the choking smoke, the three of us evacuated a second time. We drove an hour north to Portland, where the air was still clear. Friends opened their home to us and to other evacuee friends. The group spent the next three days attached to news updates as we watched the massive cloud of smoke rise above the mountains and shear to the west. We did not know the fate of our cabin, or the whereabouts of our North Fork friends and neighbors.

Air quality in western Oregon worsened. Seeming apocalyptic, the air quality index in Salem registered as high as 556. Eight miles to the southeast, the town of Turner hit 701 (levels above 150 are deemed unhealthy, while readings between 300 and 500 are considered hazardous).[7] For days, national news reports called western Oregon's air quality the worst on the planet.[8]

After two days in Portland, we headed for home, borrowed an industrial-sized air purifier from a friend's construction company, and stuffed towels under doorways; despite our efforts, still we cleaned ash from surfaces inside the house. Hazardous smoke persisted in Salem and the Willamette Valley for two more weeks.

TUESDAY, SEPTEMBER 29, 2020

Like other North Fork property owners, we weren't allowed to travel up the canyon for more than two weeks because of fallen trees, downed power lines, and damaged roads. Thankfully, we learned that Harriet's home survived the fire, but we still did not know the fate of our Elkhorn cabin. When residents were finally allowed in, my daughter Rachael and I made the first trip up together.

For the first half of the 40-mile trip from Salem, the landscape looked like it always had in the early fall: golden farm fields, yellow and orange leaves, and the Cascade mountains rising ahead to the east. We knew this route well. I'd been going to the cabin all my life—almost seventy years—and Rachael had made her first trip to the cabin in 1974 when she was just a few months old. As we entered the edge of the fire zone at Mehama, we began to see dramatic changes. We drove past groves of trees standing black and lifeless. Several homes lay in rubble.

As we turned off the main highway and headed up North Fork Road, we passed the area where I had talked with colleagues just hours before the fire came through. The Oregon Department of Forestry office was gone, reduced to a cement foundation and twisted metal roofing. A burned-out car stood on its steel axles, its tires burned away and alloy wheels melted into silver puddles. It was hard to look—and we still had 15 miles to go to reach our cabin at the center of the burn. From here on, the vibrant colors of fall turned to black and white.

A mile up the road, we watched anxiously for the familiar oak grove and the old Oakdale School. Just a few years earlier I had learned all about the old one-room school as I researched North Fork history and felt a close connection to it. Instead, we found only a pile of debris where the school had stood, arched over by scorched oaks.

Although a few scattered homes along the route remained standing, we began to realize that more cabins and homes were gone than had survived. Where there had been towering evergreens with vine maple, huckleberry, and sword fern underneath, now there was nothing green. Sunlight that shown through the burnt forest revealed rocky blackened earth.

We drove by piles of logs that had been cleared from the roadway after the fire. Stumps beside the road still smoldered, sending whisps of blue smoke into the air. We slowed many times to drive through dips in the road that had formed when culverts underneath the pavement had melted. It seemed at times that every tree in the forest had burned. The air smelled of burnt wood. Douglas-firs more than 150 feet tall stood black from top to bottom. With so many landmarks gone, it was hard at times to tell where we were along the road.

Near the Elkhorn Valley Golf Course, just five miles from the cabin, our eyes opened wide as we entered an area where groups of trees had survived and where only the undergrowth had burned. Rachael spotted a deer. These tall evergreens began to feel like the forest we knew so well.

Crossing a bridge over the North Fork, we pulled over to look down into the water. We expected the river to be discolored and full of debris, but with surprise and gratitude, we saw that it flowed crystal clear with the same green tint it had had for as long as we could remember. We saw a dozen large Chinook salmon holding in the deep pool below—a sign of something normal. The clear waters of the North Fork, the salmon, and the green trees nearby gave us reason to hope; there might be more areas of unburned forest ahead. Perhaps Elkhorn was spared the worst.

Our optimism quickly faded as the forest again turned black. Approaching Salmon Falls, we came upon enormous trees lying on the ground pointing west, some of them splintered into kindling. We could see that ferocious winds had ripped them from the ground during the firestorm, leaving their massive roots pointing to the sky. Some burning trees had fallen across the road, melting grooves in the asphalt.

As we came over the rise toward our small community, we got our first close-up look at the mountains that climb abruptly from the valley near our cabin. The dense forests had burned from the highest mountain peaks all the way to the valley floor, nearly 3,000 vertical feet. Arriving at Elkhorn, it looked as if a hurricane of fire had blown through the narrow canyon, throwing trees to the ground and turning the land black. We didn't talk much. We barely recognized anything.

Weaving our way around fallen trees, we drove as far as the Elkhorn bridge, but downed trees and power lines blocked the remaining quarter mile to our property. We walked the last stretch along the narrow dirt road, carrying water, some food, and a handsaw. We slowly cut our way through the tangle, climbing through the jumble of burnt and downed trees. Our faces, hands, and clothes quickly blackened like coal miners'. We passed the driveways of deserted properties, one by one. Each of our friends and neighbors' homes and cabins were gone, burned to the ground, some covered with piles of twisted metal, others with only their brick chimneys standing. We spotted pieces of household debris eerily lodged in the high branches of dead trees, apparently lifted by turbulent winds. We found a blackened page of a book that had been carried by the wind from someone's scorched house. Everything stood in silence.

We approached our property and struggled to locate our cabin as we looked through the charred and shattered forest. We wanted to see it standing there, as always. Finally, we spotted our old 14-foot-high steel water tank—the only recognizable landmark in our view—and there was no cabin beside it. Without words, we stood together among the burnt and broken trees. Our cabin was gone, just like the many towering Douglas-firs, homes, and cabins we had passed on our way. As time passed, we would learn more about the fire and observe more changes in the landscape. But for now, what we saw was dramatic, raw, and hard to comprehend.

The canyon we both knew and loved had been transformed in one night, barely resembling the place we had known for so long. My thoughts jumped back and forth between my memories from years past and the reality of what I now saw.

1
River Boy

I began to roam the lands of the Little North Santiam River, known to locals as the North Fork, when my parents bought a rustic cabin along the river at Elkhorn in 1954. I was three. In those early years I explored the river, valley, and forests near the cabin until I knew nearly every trail, every bend in the river, and all the best fishing holes. As I grew older, I journeyed out a bit farther, climbing peaks surrounding the river canyon where I could see more mountains in the distance, and scrambled out to explore them.

As predictable as my Mennonite family's prayers at dinner time, our Friday afternoon sojourns to the cabin typically began shortly after Dad arrived home from work as linotype operator and co-owner of a local print shop in Salem. Mom had packed food for the weekend in Dad's handcrafted wooden boxes with rope handles, and my brother John and I helped load our car. The four of us ventured out in the eight-cylinder red Buick sedan for the remote community of homes and cabins along the North Fork in the mountains east of Salem.

Getting to Elkhorn was nearly a two-hour trip in those days, almost twice as long as today. From home in west Salem, we crossed the Willamette River, drove east through town and into the countryside. Oregon's widened and straightened Santiam Highway 22 had not yet been completed in the mid-1950s, so our route crisscrossed country roads through farms and woodlands. We made a sharp turn in the small town of Sublimity then continued on through more pastures and through groves of majestic oak. Approaching the Cascade foothills, agriculture transitioned to forest as we headed east along the winding road to Mehama.

We typically stopped at the tiny Mehama Post Office to collect mail for Agnes Wheeler, a middle-aged neighbor who lived alone near our cabin. She didn't drive, so she arranged for us to get her mail whenever

we came up. She came to count on this favor and deeply appreciated the predictable delivery service. For my part, I was learning what it meant to be a neighbor.

We turned off onto North Fork Road and soon the macadam ended, often with a sudden bump (macadam was the name my family often used for pavement back then). The sound beneath the car turned to grinding and vibrating as we bounced along the rough gravel road. We passed the old Oakdale School and before long got our first look at the stunningly clear water of the North Fork. The color of the river always reminded me of an old green 7-Up bottle—so clear we could see all the rocks on the bottom, even in the deepest pools. Summers were hot and dry and the road got so dusty by late summer that all the beautiful trees along the road turned a dusty gray. When we encountered an occasional car or log truck on the narrow road, Dad applied the brakes and eased toward the shoulder as the rest of us cranked up the windows until the dust cloud cleared.

As the road began climbing, we left the farm fields and carved our way into the shady evergreen forest. In winter, the road often turned muddy and was sometimes impassable. A little farther along, we crossed Lomkers Bridge—a heavy wood-timbered structure built to serve the canyon's rustic ranches and homesteads.

As the canyon grew deeper and narrower, the road often became cluttered with rocks, holes and bumps. Sometimes the road seemed more like an obstacle course than a road. Dad watched closely as he wove in and out to avoid bottoming out or puncturing a tire. I'm sure I knew the terms "washboard" and "pothole" by the time I was five.

We passed through dense forests and groves of giant Douglas-fir trees. In places, the road bank dropped abruptly to the river. With no seatbelts in the 1950s, John and I were free to shift around in the back seat to look out the windows left and right. Sometimes looking down the steep bank was a little scary, and we hoped that Dad knew not to get too close to the edge.

We traveled a brief section of road where the ground once again flattened out near a popular landmark: an enormous beehive-shaped rock that stood up out of the ground alongside the road with a huge hole in its side, like a doorway. Some called it Wonder Rock, but we knew it as

Facing page: Agnes Wheeler's house and fish ponds, 1964. Wild rainbow trout made their home in this small creek. Mrs. Wheeler created several ponds within the rushing waters that made perfect habitat for the rainbows, and they gathered there in large numbers. (*Photo from author's collection.*)

King Tut's Tomb. The cavern inside was said to contain hidden treasures. We sometimes stopped to explore it, and although we never found the rumored treasures, we always found adventure.

A bit farther, we emerged from the forest again and began to see large open fields, a farmhouse, and a big barn nestled in the wide-open Elkhorn Valley that felt like a place under the big skies of Montana. We could look out across the fields to the surrounding mountains. When they were draped in winter snow, it was enchanting.

We passed the Cranberry House, a big red farmhouse. I never knew where it got its name but always assumed it was because of its bright red color. After crossing another bridge, we reentered the forest and passed an abandoned sawmill. With rusting metal roof and collapsing walls, the mill looked like it had been deserted a long time.

Just beyond the old mill was the remote property where Lou and Laura Meyers had lived for many years, and we often stopped to see them. We knew Mr. Meyers liked to feed the deer with apples from their trees, so on autumn visits he often invited us to observe. We watched as he reached for his pocketknife, cut the apples into pieces, and tossed them to the deer. If we stood motionless, the deer came close and ate from his hand.

Below their house was a place in the river known as "The Narrows." In the fall Mr. Meyers sometimes led us down a trail lined with red- and gold-colored vine maples to view the Chinook salmon that had traveled upstream all the way from the ocean to lay their eggs. We watched them swim in a circle in the deep clear pool surrounded by solid rock walls, awaiting higher water to assist their passage to their upstream spawning sites. Sometimes it looked as if there were hundreds of those magnificent fish in the pool.

Past the Meyers' place, the canyon narrowed again, leaving barely enough room for a road between the steep mountainside and the river. Just a half mile from the cabin we passed Salmon Falls, another major natural feature. We often pulled off and walked the trail through towering Douglas-firs to the big pool at the base of the falls. When the river ran high in winter, the sound of the falls roared through the forest.

The final attraction before reaching the cabin lay just beyond the falls. Dropping off mail to Mrs. Wheeler meant the chance to visit her trout-filled pool along Darling Creek, which flowed through her backyard. We parked the car on the side of the road, opened the wire gate of her tall fence that kept the deer out of her garden, and trekked the long path to her door. She didn't see a lot of visitors, so she always insisted that we stay for a bit. We waited for the highly anticipated question, "Would you boys like to feed the fish?" With our eager response, she opened her screened cooler on the back porch and pulled out several slices of day-old bread that she had been saving for us. Standing beside the creek, we broke the bread into pieces and tossed them one by one into one of the creek's large pools. Captivated, we watched the fish thrash the water and compete for their prize.

With fish well fed and grown-up conversations completed, Dad pulled ahead the final distance to a parking turnout where we could see our cabin across the river. In those years, the log bridge to our side of the river was often washed out by high water, so we had an alternate way to cross: by raft.

Just below the road awaited our handmade wooden raft tethered to a large alder tree with a heavy chain. Constructed of large cedar logs and kept on course by a steel cable strung to the other bank, the raft had thick wood planks spiked across the top for decking. After loading our supplies, Mom, John, and I climbed aboard as Dad brought a long Douglas-fir pole out from behind a tree where it had been stored from the previous trip. He released the raft from the chain and jumped onboard, pushing off from the bank. In Huck Finn style, he poled us across. I can still hear the pole bumping against the rocks on the river bottom as we crossed. I would sometimes lie on my stomach and watch through the clear water, hoping to spot a crawdad or rainbow trout.

The cabin was built with local materials of postwar 1940s: rough-sawn board siding, river stone, fireplace brick, and wavy Depression-era glass. Surrounded by tall Douglas-fir trees, it was a classic cabin in the woods. Mountains surrounded us, and the North Fork made a continuous roar—soft riffles in summer, loud rapids in winter, like a giant seashell held to your ear.

The cabin was all one room except for the small bathroom in one corner. A bar with tall wooden stools separated the kitchen from the rest of the cabin. John and I slept on bunk beds downstairs, and Mom and Dad slept in the loft, reached by a steep ladder. Two big front windows looked out over the river. A fireplace in the main room and the wood-burning cooking stove in the kitchen provided heat.

Our family didn't hunt or use guns, but we kept the large deer antlers and an old Winchester rifle hanging above the fireplace, left there by the previous cabin owners. One winter someone broke into the cabin and the only thing they stole was the old rifle.

With no commercial electricity in the canyon in the 1950s, we had a noisy gas-powered generator that Dad called "the power plant." Once he got it running, Dad could turn on the electric pump that brought water up from the river into the 14-foot-high steel tank that stood next to the cabin. It took the tank about ten minutes to fill before it overflowed out of a pipe on the top. When it was full, it provided gravity-pressured water for

Crossing the North Fork on the raft, c. 1954. My dad, left; my mom, middle; and my big brother (John), right. I'm standing in front of my mom. Raft crossings were possible only during the summer and fall when river levels were low. Cables to keep the raft on course are visible at top of photo. (*Photo from author's collection.*)

the kitchen sink and bathroom. In those years, we drank water from the river without treatment, and people often said it was the best water they ever tasted.

Without a radio or TV, homegrown music often provided evening entertainment. Mom sometimes played and sang hymns on our old pump organ that sat prominently in the cabin. I can still hear the rhythmic thumping of the foot pedals and the clicking of the keys that accompanied her joyful song about the beautiful stream:

> O have you not heard of that beautiful stream
> That flows through our Father's land?
> Its waters gleam bright in the heavenly light
> And ripple o'er golden sand.
>
> —Richard Torrey Jr. (1864)

On the front deck of the cabin, a large bell stood on top of a 5-foot steel pole. Originally mounted on a steam locomotive, the bell had become part of the spirit of our place. Pulling on a rope, we rang the bell upon arriving as a way of letting neighbors know we were "home." We also rang it as a farewell for departing friends as they crossed the river and passed the cabin on their way home.

As evening came to the canyon, Dad turned on the power plant for a while to run the lights. They flickered as the primitive generator rumbled and sputtered. At first light of morning, I woke up to the sound of Dad chopping wood outside. Before I had even rubbed the sleep from my eyes, there was a fire in the cookstove and Mom was fixing breakfast. There were no modern appliances in the kitchen—just the sink and wood cookstove. There was no refrigerator, only a screened cooler on the back porch. We stored a few things like a glass bottle of milk in a metal bucket submerged in the cold river. Mom cooked on the woodstove top or oven, and we ate together sitting on the bar stools. With one of the water pipes passing through the woodstove, we had hot water for washing dishes.

Dad taught my brother and me to fly-fish for rainbow trout when we were young. We fished right down from the cabin, off the anchored raft, or upstream along a trail old-timers referred to as "an old Indian trail." When walking upstream, we left the trail and walked along the edge of the

The Elkhorn cabin. Through most of my life, sunlight filtered through towering Douglas-firs, casting shadows across our cabin in the woods. (*Photo by author.*)

river, jumping from boulder to boulder. Some days when the light was just right, we saw big salmon hiding in deep pools.

Sometimes we hiked up the mountain behind the cabin on a steep narrow dirt road that took us to a clearing where the trees had been cut some years earlier. Wildlife trails showed us where the deer and other wildlife passed through, and tall black stumps deep in the woods told us that fires had burned here long ago. On hot summer days, the air smelled like dry Douglas-fir needles and in winter like the wet moss in a deep dripping forest. At night the sky was very dark (no one had outdoor lights in those days) and the stars shone brightly through the trees. On calm nights away from the sound of the river, the forest was silent.

Weekends at the cabin drew to a close on Saturday afternoons as we headed home to clean up and prepare for Sunday morning at the Spring Valley Community Church west of Salem. Raised in a Mennonite community in Minnesota, my parents brought their commitment to community service with them to Oregon; Dad served as lay pastor and Mom played the pump organ for the nondenominational services. I suppose I might have wondered why we couldn't stay at the cabin for the whole weekend, but missing Sunday services was never an option, nor anything I ever actually wished for—it was just how it was. The only time I remember being at Elkhorn on a Sunday was when my parents welcomed the entire congregation of twenty-five or thirty people to the cabin for the annual out-of-doors church service.

Before leaving the cabin, we wrote in the guest book—actually more of a journal—in which visitors and our family recorded who had come to the cabin on each trip, along with wildlife sightings and descriptions of fishing expeditions and canyon explorations. These notes provided a treasured record of our experiences at the cabin through the years.

> What a grand time in God's Great Outdoors. (Gramma Franz, July 24, 1956).
> Hiked to Cedar Creek Forest and Opal Lake, picked huckleberries. (Dad, August 5, 1961).

As I traveled up the North Fork all those years of my youth, I was connecting to the natural world in ways I didn't realize; I was falling in love with the canyon—and the outdoors in general. The mountains, the towering forests, the old trails, the North Fork's crystalline waters, our gracious neighbors, and the rustic cabin all became part of my life. These experiences influenced me in lasting and meaningful ways. My friendships, interests, and career were shaped by them.

My brother John (*right*) and me fishing from the raft at Elkhorn, c. 1957. The raft served as an ideal fishing platform as well as a shaded shelter for the young trout beneath. (*Photo from author's collection.*)

2
Out and Back

Entering my twenties, my experiences in the mountains and forests along the North Fork lured me to explore outward. I began to travel to parks, forests, and other wildlands in Oregon and across the west, hiking and camping whenever I could. The more I saw, the more I wanted to learn about the natural world.

After attending Seattle Pacific College for a year, I transferred to the University of Oregon, where I focused on my growing interest in geology. Learning about the glacier-crowned volcanoes of Oregon intrigued me, but unsure of a career path, I stepped away from school for a while to think about what to do. I took a job in home construction and began volunteering with a local conservation group, but I soon dreamed of a conservation-related career working in forests and parks. As I ventured out to explore possibilities, opportunities came that excited me, opening a world of diverse landscapes and fascinating history. At twenty-two, I married my closest friend, Sherri—a fellow explorer—and we traveled the Northwest together. We eventually established a home in Mount Angel, a small town near Salem, where our daughter was born. Later we moved to Idaho, where I took a summer job with the US Forest Service in the Sawtooth National Recreation Area. As a young man drawn to the out-of-doors, reporting to work each day at the historic Sawtooth Valley Ranger Station felt like a dream. I worked with Forest Service managers and wilderness rangers who loved the mountains and forests like I did, and I assisted them with trail maintenance in the spectacular Sawtooth Wilderness.

I took notice of the work of interpretive rangers as they shared the history and stories of the Sawtooths with visitors through guided walks, amphitheater programs, and campfire talks. In their programs, they talked about conservation and the importance of caring for the lands of the national forests that belong to all Americans. For the first time, I recognized this was the kind of work I'd love to do someday.

The Forest Service sent me to their fire school so I would be trained and ready if needed to help with firefighting during the summer. I learned how wildfires respond to drought, mountain terrain, and wind. Instructors drilled us with the Ten Standard Firefighting Orders, a set of strict safety guidelines for wildland firefighters.[1] Learning to set up an emergency fire shelter (a high-tech aluminum foil pup tent) was sobering, realizing it would be my last resort for survival if overtaken by fire.[2]

I loved my work and we loved our home in the Sawtooths, yet my wife and I recognized the challenges of raising our young daughter in that remote part of Idaho. When an opportunity came for another seasonal job with the Forest Service in Washington state that would bring us closer to schools, medical facilities, and other services, we agreed I should go for it.

We settled in Leavenworth, Washington, where I signed on with the Wenatchee National Forest in the North Cascades east of Seattle. I began as a tree-planter. Joining a crew of outdoor-oriented young people, we planted Douglas-fir and western redcedar seedlings in areas that had recently been logged. The long hours on steep mountainsides with heavy gear was tough, but I enjoyed the physical challenge, camaraderie, and fresh mountain air. At home, we knew it was a good decision to move; the small community offered us all the services and opportunities our young family could wish for.

On another job with the Forest Service, I worked on a rock core drill, assisting a professional drill operator. Our task involved drilling down to extract rock samples alongside a river to determine whether the site was suitable for a new bridge. The operator, Ron, was well-matched for the job at six feet, five inches, and built like a football lineman. By comparison, I was five feet, eight inches, and 130 pounds, and it took all my focus and energy to keep up with him (we typically worked with 36-inch pipe wrenches that weighed 40 pounds each, often holding one in each hand). One cold day, we were drilling near the top of a rock ledge, high above a rain-swollen river. The temperature abruptly dropped, and the water brought to the surface by the drill formed a sheet of ice beneath our feet. We threw shovels of sand and gravel on the ice to give us steady footing, but when a piece of equipment suddenly shifted, it knocked me off balance, and I slid toward the edge of the rock. Years later, Ron recounted, "I saw you starting to go over the edge toward the flooding river, so in about half a second, I reached out, grabbed your coat at the back of your neck, and pulled you back up."

Even though we faced challenging circumstances at times, Ron and I enjoyed our months of work together, and when I reflect on it, his strong arm and fast thinking may have saved my life that day.

As summer approached that year, I started work at the Rock Creek Guard Station, a remote outpost near the Glacier Peak Wilderness. As Rock Creek guard, I was the only employee at the site. On Mondays, I drove up-canyon to the station and stayed for the week, looking after campgrounds, posting information at trailheads for hikers, and patrolling for new fire starts in the canyon. With the arrival of fall, I joined the trail crew. We built a section of trail in the backcountry and maintained several miles of the Pacific Crest Trail.

One Sunday morning I was outside our home in Leavenworth when I heard loud distant booms—like cannons fired in the far-off mountains. A few minutes later my neighbor called out to me across the meadow.

"I just heard on the radio—those rumbling noises were from Mount St. Helens. The volcano's erupting!"

It was May 18, 1980. By noon, ash filled the air as a thick gray cloud drifted east across Washington in our direction. The bright sunny day darkened as the thick cloud of volcanic ash settled over our town. The eruption changed the landscape of Mount St. Helens and the lives of many people that day—and it would soon change the course of my life too.

Within six months of the eruption, I accepted my first permanent job with the US Forest Service at the soon-to-become Mount St. Helens National Volcanic Monument. I launched what became my long career as an interpretive ranger, working at the Mount St. Helens Visitor Center where I shared the history and stories related to the volcano with visitors through guided walks and interpretive talks—the type of job I'd first dreamed of when working in the Sawtooths.

Meeting with geologists from the US Geological Survey, our team of interpretive rangers learned the complex story of the 1980 eruption that involved a powerful lateral explosion, a massive rock-debris avalanche, an ash plume that circled the earth, and mudflows that plugged local rivers.

We set up temporary visitor centers where masses of visitors converged on western Washington to see the volcano and learn about the eruption.

Fifty-seven people lost their lives in the eruption, and I met some families of those who perished. As family members told me their stories, I felt their deep pain and loss. I met others who lost homes and cabins near the mountain and still others who felt personal loss when the youth camps and recreation sites they had enjoyed through their lives were lost.

I talked with some who barely escaped the eruption. One man showed me his spectacular photos from close to the volcano as the eruption began and described how he and his friends narrowly escaped from the eruption impact area.

When I made my first trips to the eruption area in early 1981, the landscape appeared lifeless. Trees had been shattered by the volcanic blast and ash covered everything. President Jimmy Carter visited the area soon after the eruption and compared it to the surface of the moon. Most early observers thought it would take many years for plants and animals to return because they would have to migrate many miles from outside the eruption area.

Yet ecologists who studied the changed landscape shared their surprising findings with our team; in some areas, plant roots had found protection deep in the soil while, in other places, plants and even small trees had survived beneath a cover of lingering spring snow. Elsewhere, life survived in the cold, sometimes ice-covered water of mountain lakes. From these islands of survival within the vast eruption impact area, we watched in amazement as life emerged and spread, turning the gray landscape green again—much sooner than scientists had anticipated. I came to understand that, in the natural world, nothing stays the same for very long.

Although the Mount St. Helens area was designated as a national volcanic monument in 1982, it was located within the boundaries of the Gifford Pinchot National Forest, where logging and reforestation were still routine. Within these surrounding forests, our team learned how new timber harvest areas were laid out with guidelines for protecting wildlife, watersheds, and cultural resources.[3]

Foresters took us to an old-growth forest where wildlife specialists summoned a pair of endangered northern spotted owls by imitating their calls. In response, these stunning brown birds—with wingspans of nearly 4 feet—flew in silently, perched nearby, and seemed to watch us with curiosity as we learned about efforts to protect their habitat. On other field trips we watched as large logs were placed in streams to help shade the water, retain nutrients, and provide hiding places for fish. We learned about mycorrhizal fungi that form mutually beneficial relationships between the roots of trees and other plants. I was beginning to learn about complex forest ecosystems and forest health.

One summer day our team traveled with archaeologists to a cave where researchers had uncovered animal bones and stone tools dating back more than 7,000 years.[4] I had visited ancient cultural sites in Arizona and New Mexico in years past and learned the importance of protecting them as part of our country's history, but I'd never seen a place like this in the Pacific Northwest. Sitting quietly in the subdued light of the cave after others had left, I imagined life thousands of years ago and recognized even more profoundly the importance of protecting cultural resources like this.

Several times during my years at Mount St. Helens, I joined the firefighting ranks, assisting the fire information officers on large forest fires. During these assignments, I joined planning meetings early each morning to gather updates on fire size, weather forecasts, resources working the fire (hand crews, dozers, helicopters, and so on), safety concerns, and more. It was my job to synthesize information and share it with local residents and the media. I got a good look at the challenging work of managing fires, especially one year when numerous fires stretched resources thin and managers couldn't get all the help they needed.

Through my years at Mount St. Helens, not only did I witness numerous eruptions of ash and steam that vented upward, I also watched as the volcano erupted a very thick type of lava. Rather than flowing out from the volcano, as many people might imagine, the lava was so paste-like it piled up to form a lava dome within the eruption-formed crater. Year by year we watched the dome grow larger, beginning to rebuild the mountain.

Even through my extraordinary experiences at Mount St. Helens, I faced personal challenges too. Diagnosed with cancer at age thirty-four, I had to step away from work for nearly a year. Facing surgery and months of treatment, the prospects felt daunting, until one of my cousins encouraged me: "Remember the story you've been sharing with visitors at Mount St. Helens all these years—the story of disturbance and renewal. This story will be true for you, too."

And it was. The metaphor encouraged me, and I made a full recovery.

With fresh energy, I carved out time to complete my bachelor's degree with a focus in environmental studies from The Evergreen State College in Olympia, Washington. Then another disturbance came when my marriage ended suddenly and my life was pulled apart. As I processed that change, a new opportunity arose.

After more than twenty years with the Forest Service, I was offered the chance to transfer to the National Park Service at Hawai'i Volcanoes National Park on the Big Island of Hawai'i to manage the Kīlauea Visitor Center and join its team of interpretive rangers. The move to the islands opened me to a new landscape, a new place of work, and a new way of life. Hawaiian coworkers and neighbors welcomed me from the day I arrived, helping me settle and learn my way around. Hawai'i is the most culturally diverse region in the United States; it seemed everyone was welcome on the Big Island no matter where they came from, their family ancestry, or individual differences. I felt renewed in Hawai'i's aloha spirit of love and caring.[5]

I went to work with the park's team of interpretive rangers and dove into learning about the Hawaiian volcanoes. Geologists taught us about the nearly continuous eruptions at Kīlauea volcano as they walked us along ribbons of flowing red lava. This type of lava hadn't erupted in Oregon for more than a thousand years, yet here I was standing within inches of it in Hawai'i and even feeling its heat through my boots. It led me to feel more connected than ever to Oregon's volcanic areas that had erupted the same kinds of lava long ago.

Hawaiian cultural practitioners told stories of volcanic eruptions preserved through their oral history and recited in ancient chants and hula. The accounts of science and oral history coincided exactly, telling the same island history from different perspectives.

I recall the first time I watched ancient hula performed on the rim of Kīlauea volcano next to the vents releasing volcanic steam. Hawaiian dancers wore skirts and head leis made from the green leaves and fibers of native plants and danced to the rhythm of a traditional drum fashioned from a hollowed gourd. A powerful voice called out the chant as dancers moved in unison and steam rose around them. Feeling the emotional power of the dance in that lava-covered landscape gave me "chicken skin," a term used in Hawai'i for goose bumps.

On days off, I traveled to Hawaiian cultural sites where I learned about traditional shoreline villages. I walked rainforest trails surrounded by tree ferns and Hawaiian ʻōhiʻa lehua trees, adorned with brightly colored red and yellow blooms. I observed rare Hawaiian birds like the ʻiʻiwi, a vermilion-red bird with black wings and a gracefully curving pink bill. Swimming in the Pacific surf, I encountered endangered green sea turtles. Walking among ancient petroglyphs I learned about life on the island in centuries past. I hiked across expansive lava fields at night with a head lamp to stand next to red-hot lava flowing across the land from Kīlauea Volcano. I watched as the lava poured into the Pacific Ocean, creating tall columns of steam in the night sky, tinted orange by the glow of lava.

In daylight, I often walked on hard black lava covering areas that had once been thriving communities of homes, churches, and schools. Sometimes a lone street sign or short section of paved road appeared in the middle of vast lava fields, the only evidence of communities at those locations in years past. I worked with and became friends with people whose lives had been dramatically affected by these lava flows and witnessed their resolve to move forward and rebuild on the impermanent landscape.

I observed the love Hawaiians hold for their island home as local musicians sang countless songs about the beauty of Hawaiʻi. I visited local art galleries filled with paintings and photographs displaying Hawaiian forests, birds, beaches, and the spectacular erupting volcanoes. I became a regular at cultural festivals like the Big Island's Merrie Monarch hula festival that celebrated Hawaiian culture and demonstrated their commitment to perpetuating their rich history and living culture. I could not have known how observing their pride in Hawaiian history was beginning to ignite my own interest in the history of the places where I grew up back in Oregon.

Amid the beauty of Hawaiʻi, I also learned that the islands are known as the "endangered species capital of the world" because their native plants and animals—many of which are found nowhere else on earth—have been so significantly disrupted by human development and the rapid spread of invasive species. Yet I saw resource managers in the park and throughout the islands working hard—seemingly against all odds—to support the long-term survival of Hawaiʻi's native plants and animals. I watched as volunteers from around the world came to help protect beach habitat for endangered hawksbill and green sea turtles. I visited greenhouses where park botanists nurtured rare native plants to reintroduce into the wild. I caught glimpses of some of the rarest endemic Hawaiian birds that resource managers seek to protect from extinction. The passion and commitment of Hawaiians to protect their island home reinforced my long-held commitment to conservation.[6]

One summer, a lava flow from Kīlauea ignited a fire in the rain forest, big enough to require a fire team from the US mainland to help manage it. I would never have imagined a forest fire in the rain forest, but invasive grasses that dry out quickly and ignite easily became the kindling that allowed even the damp forest to burn.

By my fifth year in Hawai'i, I found myself putting down roots; it was beginning to feel like home. At the same time, I recognized that my deepest roots were back in Oregon, in the forests and volcanic mountains of my youth. When an opportunity arose, I returned to Oregon to what would become my final professional assignment: director of a new visitor center in the Tillamook State Forest with the Oregon Department of Forestry in the coastal mountains.

By this time, I had reconnected with my longtime friend Shawn, who was living in Canada. She had lived in the Willamette Valley years ago and also wanted to return. She met me in Oregon and we explored backroads and wilderness trails on our days off—and spent a lot of time up the North Fork.

At the Tillamook Forest Center, our interpretive team told the story of another historical natural event: the Tillamook Burn. A huge area northwest of Portland had been the site of four major forest fires between 1933 and 1951, described collectively as one of the largest fire events in Oregon's recorded history. I met people who remembered the burn and who fought the fires. They described daylight turning to darkness as smoke settled across the land and how difficult it was to watch their beloved forest burn. They also told of the legions of individuals who came to fight the fires including prison inmates, loggers, Civilian Conservation Corps members, and volunteers. In the aftermath of the fires, tree planters who came to help establish a new forest were joined by an unusual group of workers: busloads of school children.[7]

I talked with people who proudly expressed that they had been among the school kids who planted trees in the burn and the excitement they felt when they saw the forest begin to turn green again within a short time. One man teared up as he recalled watching newly resprouted vine maple and other native plants exhibit striking colors of red and yellow in the fall. "Whole mountainsides burst into color again. Our beautiful forest was coming back," he explained.

During my years on the Tillamook, I celebrated the birth of my grandsons. As soon as they each learned to walk, these three explorers began to trek along the North Fork, just as I had done when I was a boy, and as their mother had done as a girl. As the boys grew, we walked forest trails together, swam in the river, stood in the spray of waterfalls, and fished for rainbows in the clear waters of the North Fork.

After retiring in 2012, I realized that I knew more about the places I had lived and worked in Idaho, Washington, and Hawai'i than I had ever learned about the North Fork, the place of my youth. Inspired by experiences in my career, I set out on a path to learn the history of the place I have loved so much throughout my life.

I wrote out some of my earliest boyhood memories on the North Fork with an aim to fold them together with some of the area's history I was beginning to learn. I imagined writing for family and friends and a few North Fork neighbors, but when the North Santiam Historical Society invited me to speak at a public event and a room full of local residents packed in to hear it, I realized there was broader interest in North Fork stories than I had imagined. The idea for a book was born.

Time disappeared as I immersed myself in websites, museums, and libraries. I discovered old maps, newspapers, and countless books—many out of print. A throng of geologists, archaeologists, and many other experts shared information about the North Fork canyon that was not available in published literature. Knowledge keepers with the Confederated Tribes of Grand Ronde and the Confederated Tribes of Siletz Indians generously offered stories and insights I could never have gathered from any other source. Longtime canyon residents—many in their eighties and nineties—recounted stories, uncovered dusty family scrapbooks, and shared many cups of coffee as they revealed untold elements of canyon history. In all, nearly a hundred individuals offered firsthand information.

I learned that the human history of the canyon reached back thousands of years, far deeper than I could have imagined. My fondness for this river and its canyon grew ever deeper.

In 2020, as I neared completion of my research and writing, the Beachie Creek Fire exploded along the North Fork. Change came instantly and powerfully to the canyon and its people. As my family and I began to address the many challenges brought by the fire, another personal challenge erupted into my life when I received diagnosis of another type of cancer—and it would be more challenging than anything I had faced before. Plans for rebuilding the cabin and finishing this book abruptly stopped as I once again centered my energy on healing and regaining health. Family and friends rallied around me, offering encouragement and support. Following surgery and treatments, favorable medical reports allowed me to refocus. With unanimous agreement, our family finalized plans to rebuild the cabin, and I set out to complete my manuscript.

Beautiful Stream chronicles the broad scope of North Fork history, including elements of my own "out and back" journey. My early years along the North Fork gave me the footing to move out to the path of my career, and then my career experiences steered me right back to the North Fork to learn and share its story.

3
Volcanoes, Glaciers, and Ancient Lakes

SEPTEMBER 2012—A QUIET EVENING AT ELKHORN

I had just climbed the ladder to the sleeping loft and clicked off the lights for the night. At ten o'clock it was pitch dark and stone-quiet in the cabin when I closed my eyes. I was barely asleep when I was awakened by the sound—the likes of which I had never heard before.

It rumbled like a big truck traveling up North Fork Road with a load of huge boulders bumping around in the back. But why was someone working so late? How could a truck be heading straight for the cabin when the road is on the other side of the river? My eyes popped open as I suddenly realized it couldn't possibly be a truck.

Bam! The earthquake hit. It was as if the truck had slammed into the cabin.

I bolted out of bed and listened as the rumbling continued on past the cabin, as if the truck had passed right through the building. For a few moments—ten or twelve seconds maybe—the cabin rocked back and forth, twisting and creaking. As quickly as it began, the rumbling diminished and the shaking stopped. Silence again filled the dark cabin.

I'd felt earthquakes many times before, especially while living on the flank of Kīlauea volcano and working at Hawai'i Volcanoes National Park, but I'd never felt one at the cabin, nor had I heard the sound of rocks moving in the earth that I had mistaken for a truck. I learned the next day it had been a 3.5 magnitude quake centered near the town of Molalla, about 30 miles northwest of the cabin. Although it was not large or damaging, people felt the quake for more than a hundred miles around.[1]

Reflecting on that evening and my years at Mount St. Helens and Hawai'i Volcanoes National Park, I'm awed by the powerful earth forces that have shaped the planet over millions of years. In some places, volcanoes have erupted and built massive mountains while landslides have pulled mountains down. Earthquakes have dramatically shifted the surface of the earth, and glaciers have ground mountains down and reshaped them. These events are still happening across the globe and make national and international news as they continue to shape the surface of the planet.

Since I was young, I have understood that volcanoes built Oregon's Cascade mountains, and that Mount Hood in northwest Oregon is one of the most visible and well-known of those. But what about the mountains surrounding the North Fork? I had always understood they were volcanic, but what more was known about their origins? After working twenty-five years around active volcanoes, I was hungry to find out.

I started by searching the internet and absorbing all the local geology books I could find. The sources provided good background on Oregon geology, but only a few offered anything specific to the North Fork. I decided to contact friend and colleague David Sherrod, who worked for the US Geological Survey (USGS) at the Cascades Volcano Observatory in Vancouver, Washington, and who I hoped might have some leads. I had worked with David in Hawai'i when he was stationed at the Hawaiian Volcano Observatory.

David graciously welcomed me to meet at his office. When I arrived, he pulled up materials on his computer and shuffled through a set of file cabinets in the USGS archives. He disappeared for a while and reappeared with more papers. By the time I left his office, I had a bulging stack of reports and field studies under my arm and a big roll of geological maps to pack home. I had struck it rich.

Good fortune also brought me a chance meeting with a man along the North Fork. I saw his vehicle with US government plates and his equipment set up along North Fork Road near our cabin, and I could not resist stopping to say hello. I learned that he also worked for USGS and was studying landslides in our North Fork watershed! Steve Sobieszczyk (who invited me to call him Sobie) shared a bit about his research and we exchanged contact information and agreed to meet later in his Portland office. Like David, Sobie had bundles of maps and reports, and luckily for me, his work focused specifically on the North Fork canyon. He generously provided me copies of his North Fork canyon materials to take home.

Only longtime geologists like David and Sobie would have access to this much information about such a small watershed. Poring over their materials, I began to get a picture of the North Fork's geological past.

BUILT BY VOLCANOES

I learned that until about 50 million years ago there were no mountains or volcanoes where the North Fork flows today, but that the first rumblings of volcanic activity were beginning. As the first flows of molten lava erupted and covered the earth in this area, they began laying the foundation for what would become Oregon's Cascade mountains, including those that surround the North Fork.

Volcanoes continued to erupt here—perhaps intermittently—for millions of years. Some eruptions produced fluid basalt lavas that readily flowed across the land in the same way people often see Hawaiian lavas flow today. But most eruptions produced thicker lava called andesite, which was more likely to build steep-sided volcanoes like nearby Mount Jefferson and the volcanoes of the Andes Mountains, where this type of lava gets its name. These accumulations of volcanic rock built the Cascades higher and higher, including the mountains surrounding the North Fork. Since the Labor Day fire of 2020 burned so much of the forest, these seemingly countless deposits of volcanic rock have been exposed far more than before.[2]

Not all eruptions produced lava flows; some exploded violently, sending ash into the atmosphere and slurries of mud and rock down the mountainsides or deposited ash and frothy pumice across the landscape.[3] In some places, volcanoes erupted in forested areas, burying trees and plants in the deposits of ash, pumice, mud, and molten lava.

During my research, I met a North Fork resident who guided me along a section of the river where we saw pieces of petrified wood embedded in volcanic ash from those ancient eruptions. I had long looked at the canyon's five-hundred-year-old North Fork trees in amazement, but these pieces of petrified wood helped me visualize forests that grew here even longer ago, when volcanoes were still building this mountain landscape.

Even as volcanic eruptions dramatically transformed western Oregon geography by forming the early Cascade mountains, the eruptions had farther-reaching effects as well. Through countless explosive eruptions over millions of years, volcanoes blasted vast amounts of ash into the atmosphere. Prevailing winds carried much of the ash hundreds of miles east, in the same way the eruption of Mount St. Helens sent ash into eastern Washington in 1980. Over time, erosion cut into some of these deep ash layers to reveal the landscape known today as Oregon's Painted Hills. Spectacular bands of red, yellow, black, and gold create one of Oregon's most admired landscapes in central Oregon.[4]

During a recent visit to the Painted Hills, I thought back to our Santiam country volcanoes, admiring the starring role they played in creating this stunning landscape more than a hundred miles away.

Eruptions continued in the North Fork area and surrounding Santiam country until about 8 million years ago, when volcanic activity shifted to the east to form the part of the range that includes Oregon's renowned volcanoes Mount Hood, Mount Jefferson, and the Three Sisters.

Even after most of the eruptions ended in the western Cascades, one more volcano came to life at the headwaters of the North Fork, now called Battle Ax mountain. Scientists refer to it as a volcano because it is the intact remnant of the most recent volcano that erupted relatively recently in geologic time—about 1 million years ago. Hikers on the Battle Ax trail can still see segments of the actual lava flows that erupted from the volcano. By contrast, all other mountains in the North Fork canyon are built from a jumble of volcanic rocks from the much older volcanoes.[5]

GLACIERS

As Battle Ax was still erupting, the earth's climate began to cool, marking the beginning of the Great Ice Age. Glaciers grew in the Cascade Range, extending from the high mountains down into surrounding valleys, and filled all of the upper North Fork canyon. As the heavy ice masses pushed their way downslope like giant scrapers, they wore down the high mountains and scoured the valleys. They reached farthest into the valleys 20,000–25,000 years ago and melted as the glacial age ended about 12,000 years ago.[6]

I've seen evidence of glaciation in the North Fork canyon in many places. All of the upper valleys in the watershed display U-shaped profiles that are characteristic of glacially carved valleys, compared to deep, V-shaped valleys that are more typical of valleys carved by rivers. Scooped

Battle Ax Mountain from the southwest three months before the 2020 fire. (*Photo by author.*)

out by glaciers, Opal Lake and nearby Elkhorn Lake are known to geologists as cirque lakes or tarns.

THE ANCIENT LAKES OF ELKHORN

With my long interest in geology and my love of the North Fork canyon, I delighted in learning about the volcanoes and glaciers of the area. Yet for me, among the most interesting of all stories in North Fork history relates to landslides that have also played a major role in shaping life in the canyon.

I had long recognized that fast-flowing rivers in the Cascade mountains, fed by heavy rains and melting snow, carved steep-sided canyons, so I often puzzled about why there was so much relatively flat ground along the river in Elkhorn Valley. This is where Sobie's research uncovered a little-known story.

Near present-day Salmon Falls, within view of our cabin, two large landslides entered the river at some time in the prehistoric past, one from the north, the other from the south. A massive volume of rock and debris entered the river, and the resulting natural dam blocked the river's flow, creating a mile-long lake. The lake covered all of today's upper Elkhorn Valley from Salmon Falls to a point near the western boundary of the Opal Creek Scenic Area. Farther downstream, another slide entered the canyon near present-day Elkhorn Valley Recreation Site, forming a natural dam that blocked the river there. This second lake flooded the lower part of Elkhorn Valley, including the area of today's Elkhorn Valley Golf Course.[7]

Both lakes eventually filled with sediment, leaving large flat areas in their places. Geologists refer to these resulting flat areas as terraces. When I first heard this story from Sobie, I recall my amazement. The location of our cabin and nearly all the other Elkhorn homes would have been under 100 feet of water.[8]

Native Americans and homesteaders, and later golfers, campers, swimmers, homeowners, and all others who have benefited from the expansive flat Elkhorn Valley, owe it all to the history of landslides and ancient lakes.

My journey to learn the history of the North Fork began with a new understanding of how the North Fork took the form of a rugged mountain-rimmed canyon. I learned that it was here, among its volcano-built mountains, within its glacier-carved canyons, and through the nearly flat Elkhorn Valley, that humans would come to gather the North Fork's resources, admire its beauty, and—for some—make it their home.

4
Since Time before Memory

It's one of the oldest stories in Oregon. It tells that long ago a great flood covered the entire Willamette Valley, and the water rose so high that only the tallest mountains, like Marys Peak in the Coast Range, stood above it. People ran for their lives to stay above the rapidly rising waters in the safety of that high mountain. The story was told to anthropologists in the early 1900s by Kalapuya Elder William Hartless, and it is told today by the Kalapuyans—the Native people who have long made the Willamette Valley their home. Without a written language, they perfected an oral tradition that included storytelling to perpetuate their culture and document important historic events. It's not surprising that a story about a flood of this magnitude has been told over and over and passed on through countless generations.[1]

A few decades ago, geologists started to describe a series of Northwest events called the Missoula Floods that included flooding of the Willamette Valley at the end of the last ice age (12,000–15,000 years ago). I first learned about the floods during my college years. Studies concluded that a glacier blocked the flow of a fork of the Columbia River in Montana, forming a lake that filled a vast area including present-day Missoula. Over time, the ice dam formed and failed multiple times, sending cataclysmic torrents like giant tsunamis down the Columbia River toward the Pacific Ocean. Water filled the Columbia so rapidly that it could not readily pass through the narrow sections of the river's channel. Floodwaters backed up into tributaries like the Willamette River and filled what is now called the Willamette Valley with water 200 feet deep near present-day Salem, leading it to look more like Puget Sound in Washington than a broad flat valley. Retreating waters left 10–40 feet of nutrient-rich sediment in the valley bottom, creating the fertile soils that became highly valued by

Native inhabitants, settlers arriving on the Oregon Trail, and present-day farmers.[2]

The strong parallel between the Kalapuyan and Missoula Floods accounts is impossible to miss. It suggests that the Kalapuyans witnessed one or more of the Missoula Floods, a clue that Native people have lived in western Oregon for at least 12,000 years. According to Kalapuyan oral tradition, their ancestors have lived in western Oregon even longer—since time before memory. These are among the people who have come to the North Fork for thousands of years.[3]

Although I grew up in Salem, I never learned about western Oregon's Native American history. It was not taught in school, and the subject wasn't discussed anywhere else that I remember. I knew the names Santiam, Molalla, and Calapooia (also spelled Kalapuya) because they were names of western Oregon rivers, but I never understood they were connected to Native history.

On the day we celebrated the opening of the new Tillamook Forest Center in 2007, a man introduced himself to me. He was Robert Kentta, a tribal member and cultural leader at the Confederated Tribes of Siletz Indians, who had been an adviser to the Department of Forestry in development of exhibits for the new center before I came to work there. We became friends and through our conversations I learned about Native history in the Tillamook area and began hearing about the Kalapuya and Molalla people of Santiam country.

Santiam is a Native American name. First heard by early western explorers and settlers as San-ta-am, Sandy-am, or San-de-ham, over time Santiam became the widely accepted spelling. Some early American settlers understood that the name meant swift, noisy, or roaring—a good description of this powerful river.[4] I learned that Molalla and Calapooia are not only names of rivers, they are also names of local tribes. I also began to understand the linkages between these tribes and their use of the resources of the North Fork canyon. Now when I see these names, I am reminded that they have been spoken here for thousands of years.

Over time, the larger story of western Oregon's Native people and their connections to the North Fork began to unfold for me. I attended a Culture and History Summit in 2015 hosted by the Confederated Tribes of Grand Ronde. Tribal Education Department manager Eirik Thorsgard shared a huge collection of western Oregon Native history documents with me that were mostly unpublished. After reading the documents, my learning continued through conversations with Grand Ronde's Cultural Resource Manager David Harrelson. In 2023, as I neared completion of my research, Grand Ronde tribal member and scholar Dr. David Lewis published a book titled *Tribal Histories of the Willamette Valley* that confirmed and added to my knowledge.

I learned that Molallans and Kalapuyans lived in winter villages in the Willamette Valley and other lower-elevation areas but spent other times of the year hunting, fishing, and gathering resources along higher-elevation tributaries, including the North Fork.[5] Most information suggests that the Molallans were the primary users of resources in the mountains surrounding the North Fork (the town of Molalla is named for this group). The Santiam Band of the Molallas claimed territory along the upper reaches of the North and South Santiam Rivers.[6] Known as great hunters, they must have found the mountains excellent for hunting deer and elk and collecting blue huckleberries that have long been a favored food of Native people (celebrated today as First Foods).

By contrast, the Kalapuyan traditional homeland included the Willamette Valley and surrounding hills, including lands along the lower sections of streams flowing into the Willamette River. Numerous Kalapuyan tribes and bands organized themselves around various chiefs and specialized in their own foods and languages. I learned that the Santiam Band of Kalapuyas lived throughout the lower reaches of the Santiam watershed, including lands of the North and South Santiam Rivers and, like the Molallas, would have had access to resources along the North Fork.[7] Author David Lewis says that accounts from many tribes suggest that the higher-elevation areas in the Cascade Range were considered shared resource areas among the tribes.[8]

Within the North Fork canyon, physical evidence of Native use has been uncovered in many locations, including some not far from our cabin at Elkhorn. Many of the artifacts are estimated to be a thousand years old and older. Archeologists and others have found arrow points (also called arrowheads) made of black obsidian (shiny volcanic glass) and red jasper stone, as well as the small flakes of those materials that would have been left behind by the makers of arrow points and other stone tools.[9] While the red jasper points were likely made from local materials, obsidian would have had to be imported because it does not occur naturally in the North Fork watershed. Based on analysis at the Northwest Research Obsidian Studies Laboratory in Corvallis, Oregon, most of the obsidian came from the Three Sisters area, 50 miles south, while some came from Mount Jefferson, 20 miles east.

In 2018, Elkhorn friends invited me to share what I was learning about canyon history at a community gathering. After hearing my presentation, one of our neighbors told me he had an arrow point that was found nearby and invited me to his house to see it. Made from shiny black obsidian, it was intricately shaped and very beautiful. I realized I was touching a piece of North Fork history dating back a thousand years or more. Native history was all around—and I had never known it.

According to knowledge keepers at Grand Ronde and Siletz, both the Santiam Kalapuyas and Santiam Molallas lived in plankhouses typically framed with poles that supported the roof and walls. Cedar planks or thick sheets of cedar or hemlock bark served as roofing and siding. Some

Obsidian arrow point from the North Fork canyon, 2019. (*Photo by author.*)

houses were partly excavated into the ground or had earth banked up around the walls for added insulation.[10]

Santiam Kalapuyas were known to locate winter villages near the confluences of the Willamette River and its tributaries. One such village was called Chemeketa, location of present-day Salem. To the southeast, a prized winter village known as Anhalpum was at the confluence of the North and South Santiam, a short distance from today's towns of Stayton and Scio.[11] Santiam Molallas had a village at Crooked Finger Prairie, southeast of the town of Molalla.[12] Early settlers reported that the "Santiam Indians" had a village along the North Santiam River and kept the valley burned to favor camas. The open areas made it easy for settlers to transform the land into farms. The report does not indicate whether it was a Molalla or Kalapuya village.[13] No winter villages are known to have been located in the North Fork canyon.

Some years after we met, Robert Kentta honored me with an invitation to attend a Siletz community Feather Dance at their plankhouse on the Siletz Reservation. I had never seen a western Oregon plankhouse and certainly had never seen a traditional western Oregon Native dance. I found that the dance not only helped me understand more about Native history, it also connected me directly to current cultural traditions of some of western Oregon's Native people. Although I knew very little about western Oregon's Native history at that time, the tangible experience at the plankhouse affected all of my senses and kindled my desire to learn even more about the history of Oregon's Native people.

In recent years, the Confederated Tribes of Grand Ronde built a large ceremonial plankhouse on tribal land at Grand Ronde. Named Achaf-hammi ("house made of cedar planks" in the Tualatin Kalapuyan language), it is used as a community house for gatherings and ceremonies. Tribal members open it to the public several times each year for special events to share their stories and traditions.[14]

I first visited Achaf-hammi in 2016 during a community event. Approaching the plankhouse on a rainy evening, I entered the round front doorway and immediately smelled smoke from a large wood fire built in the center of the earthen floor. The subdued light and log and cedar plank interior drew me in as I watched the fire's smoke escape through an opening in the roof. One of the tribal members blessed the meal of elk stew, roasted camas, baked salmon, and huckleberry pie in a Native language that I had never heard spoken before. A group of men sat in a circle drumming and singing traditional songs in their language as I stood in line to receive the meal. Following dinner, our hosts shared more drumming, singing, and dancing, including a friendship song.

In the 1970s, archaeologists excavated a site just east of the Kalapuya village of Chemeketa near the I-5 interchange at State Highway 22 in Salem. They found projectile points for arrows, pestles, and stone bowl fragments, hammerstones, and other stone tools. Research indicates this was an extensive food processing site that included rock-lined earth ovens for baking camas lily bulbs that were used as much as 5,600 years ago. Evidence of hazelnut, onion, acorn, and cherry processing was also found there.[15] Since this site is within the territory of the Santiam Kalapuyas, it gives an idea of how long they and their ancestors may have gathered resources within the North Fork canyon.

While other sites scattered through Santiam country have been found to date back as many as 8,000 years, archaeologist and Confederated Tribes of Grand Ronde tribal member Don Day told me that he and some other tribal members believe even older sites lay buried beneath deep layers of Missoula Flood sediment.[16]

Like other Native people in the Northwest, the Santiam Kalapuyas and Santiam Molallas traveled the region in well-established seasonal circuits or "rounds" in spring, summer, and fall, stopping at established camps to gather resources. These seasonal rounds are believed to have been practiced in western Oregon for more than 8,000 years.[17]

I had first learned of seasonal rounds while working at Mount St. Helens. I recall Cowlitz Indian Tribal elder Maryann Lewis, who worked with us at the Mount St. Helens Visitor Center, told me about her ancestors going on summer trips into the mountains to gather huckleberries. Forest Service archaeologists shared information about artifacts they found around Mount St. Helens, providing evidence of a long Native history. I had often wondered whether there was Native history in the Willamette Valley and in Santiam country similar to what Maryann Lewis told me about Mount St. Helens. Now I know.

In spring, both the Molallans and Kalapuyans gathered camas bulbs and other early-season foods. Harvesters dug the bulbs, growing in abundance throughout the Willamette Valley and Santiam country, with a specialized digging stick and roasted them in earth-ovens. Some

Achaf-hammi plank house at Grand Ronde, Oregon. (*Photo by author.*)

camas was pounded into condensed "cakes" and stored for winter use and trade.[18]

In April each year, I drive across Salem to the Oregon State Fairgrounds to see the brilliant fields of blooming camas flowers that still grow in abundance there. As I walk among these fields of blue, I think of the reports of early Willamette Valley settlers describing the large fields of blue camas flowers that reminded them of lakes of blue water.

As spring progressed, the Molallans and Kalapuyans left their winter village sites and moved into the hills and lower canyons of the Cascades in family groups to fish, hunt, dig higher-elevation camas, and gather other materials. At this time of year some groups would have entered the North Fork canyon. Remembering the seasonal round, I now watch for the patches of camas that still bloom in May within the lower North Fork canyon.

Early in my research, I was invited to join Oregon tribal members on a late spring field trip to harvest camas. I met the diverse group that included members from various western Oregon tribes, a land manager from the Bureau of Land Management (BLM), and several other guests like me who had come to learn about western Oregon's Native history and traditional Native use of camas. We boarded a school bus and started up the bumpy roads into the coastal mountains. Arriving at the camas field, we learned about the cooperative effort between tribal members and BLM to restore this high-quality camas site with annual burning to keep it free from encroaching shrubs and trees. Using traditional digging sticks, we dug bulbs from various locations in the field rather than digging all from one spot, thereby assuring regrowth of plants throughout the site. We learned not to harvest a bulb from a plant with a white blossom because plants with white flowers are extremely poisonous—known widely as death camas. We had to be careful how we pushed the stick into the ground to be sure we didn't damage the bulb. That evening, we gathered to talk about our experience. Tribal members served us samples of baked camas that they had prepared for us in advance. We all delighted in the flavor, reminiscent of a baked pear or sweet potato.

By mid- and late summer, people historically traveled to the upper canyons to gather resources such as blue huckleberries. They circulated through customary sites where they assembled temporary structures or, in good weather, slept in the open.[19] A site near Jawbone Flats area in the upper canyon of the North Fork has been identified as a possible former summer Molalla or Kalapuya camp site.[20] In some years, Native people burned high-elevation huckleberry areas after harvest to reinvigorate the berry patches and keep unwanted trees and brush from encroaching, thereby ensuring continued high-quality habitat for this important food resource.

When weather cooled, they moved back to lower-elevation areas to gather late-season foods such as hazel nuts and wapato (an aquatic plant with a potato-like tuber). They also harvested acorns from extensive oak groves in the valley and prepared for winter. Oregon tribal members continue to gather resources from the land, including some for traditional uses such as weaving and carving, and some for use in ceremonies.

Returning to their villages in the fall, Kalapuyans also managed camas fields by annual burning. Like the management of huckleberry areas, burning the camas areas prevented trees, shrubs and other plants from taking over the prized camas fields. Other valued resources, such as berries and forage for deer and elk, also benefited from the burning. These routine horticultural practices maintained open prairies in the Willamette Valley—the very open land that lured American settlers to the area.[21]

While resources were abundant, they were not evenly distributed across the region. For this reason, tribes actively traded in a highly developed economic system. To facilitate trade, tribal groups developed a universal intertribal trade language called chinuk wawa that allowed for communication between people who spoke drastically different languages; chinuk wawa (also known as Chinook Jargon) is taught today at the Grand Ronde Reservation.[22] This is the language I had heard that night at the plankhouse event.

Native people had full access to the North Fork through an extensive trail network. A miner and prospector journal from 1864 refers to "Old Indian Trails" along the Little North Fork, and I've seen the old Indian trails noted on early maps of the North Santiam and the North Fork. Often located along ridges, the trails provided direct access to high-quality berry fields and hunting areas, as well as water sources at higher-elevation springs and lakes.[23]

Trails stretched out across the Cascades in a far-reaching network of trade routes. Some trails were frequented by the Wasco and Wishram People from the Columbia River and the Klamath People in Southern Oregon. One historic trail across the Cascades is still known as the Klamath Trail because of its use by the Klamath Indians in centuries past. The Klamath Indians were known to use this trail to transport slaves from California to trade at sites in Oregon. One branch of the trail from Klamath country went north to the trading center at Celilo Falls on the Columbia River, while another branch turned west and crossed the Cascades south of Mount Jefferson. As the western branch crossed the mountains, it passed through the North Santiam Canyon and possibly parts of the North Fork Canyon. Modern recreation trails appear to follow some of the same routes as traditional Native trails.[24]

Oral histories of western Oregon's Native people, along with findings from archaeological research and information from many other sources show us that Native people have lived in western Oregon for countless generations. As part of their lives, they utilized the North Fork's resources extensively, coming to it repeatedly since a time before memory. My experiences holding the obsidian arrow point in my hand, attending the Feather Dance, joining the evening at the Achaf-hammi plankhouse, and digging camas and tasting its sweet and savory flavor all served to bring the history and culture of the Kalapuyan and Molallan people to life—a history dating back to a time before memory.

5
Trails of Tears

Through the years, I heard many references celebrating the American pioneers who came to the Oregon Country—in fact, I could see the giant gold-leaf figure of a pioneer man atop the state capitol building from our home in west Salem when I was young. Yet I rarely heard reference to the Native people who had lived here for so long and were displaced by the newcomers. I had no awareness of the hardships they faced when Europeans and Americans from the eastern states arrived. By the late 1700s, European sailing ships began mapping the Pacific coastline from California to British Columbia. At some locations, sailors came ashore and made contact with Native people and infected communities with rapidly spreading, deadly diseases for which the Native people had little or no immunity. Epidemics launched a devastating decline in population and upheaval in social and economic structures that had been in place for thousands of years.[1]

In 1805, Lewis and Clark arrived in what is now Oregon, followed by fur traders and then missionaries who came into the Willamette Valley and Santiam country to bring Christianity to the Native population. In 1843, the Great American Migration brought wagon trains of about a thousand American pioneers west along the new Oregon Trail. Many settled in the Willamette Valley, displacing Native people. The 1850 Donation Land Claim Act allowed white male US citizens to claim 320 acres of land (640 acres for married couples), which led to further displacement.

By this time, it is estimated that more than 90 percent of Native people in the Willamette Valley had already died from disease.[2] It's impossible to imagine what it must have been like for Native people to see their lands taken and their communities emptied.

This influx of American pioneers was happening when the land did not legally belong to the United States—these were the homelands of the

Native people. In view of this, the US government set out to make treaties with the Native people of western Oregon. I first became familiar with the western Oregon treaties when Robert Kentta gave me a copy of the book *The People Are Dancing Again* by Charles Wilkinson.

In 1851, US government officials met with local Indian chiefs of at least twenty western Oregon tribes to negotiate treaties.[3] They pushed hard for the tribal leaders to cede ownership of vast areas of land in the Willamette Valley and the Cascades, including lands of the North Santiam and the North Fork to the US government in exchange for establishment of a reservation for them east of the Cascades. None of the tribal leaders would agree to it. But with the loss of so many of their people and the increasing number of settlers arriving each year, leaders had few options.

Among the Santiam Band of the Kalapuya were three chiefs: Ti-a-can, Alquema, and Sophan. Representing the Band in treaty negotiations, Chief Alquema stated unequivocally through a translator, "We understand fully what you mean [that we should remove to east of the Cascade Mountains], and that it may be better for us, but our minds are made up. We wish to reserve this piece of land."

Alquema was pointing at an area on a map about 10 miles from the mouth of the North Fork showing lands around their village of Anhalpum. Seeking to keep this part of his homeland for the future of his people, he continued:

> We have been willing to throw away the rest of our country, and reserve the land lying between the forks of the Santiam! You thought that was too much. . . . Then we agreed to take this small piece between the Creek and North Branch. You want us still to take less. We can't do it, it is too small, it is tying us up in too small a space. We wish to reserve this piece of land. We do not want to leave it. We would rather be shot on it than to remove.[4]

Following several days of discussions, a treaty was signed on April 16, 1851, with the Santiam Band of Kalapuya Indians to create a reservation along the lower North Santiam River, including the lands between the North and South Forks of the Santiam River, in the vicinity of their

Alquema, chief of the "Santiams" Band of the Calapooya, c. 1840s. Sketch by George Gibbs. *(Courtesy of the Peabody Museum of Archaeology and Ethnology, Harvard University, 41-72-10/303. Image is a gift of the Estate of Belle J. Bushnell, 1941.)*

Anhalpum village. This may have been close to what Alquema had asked for. The three chiefs each signed the treaties with an X, agreeing to cede all other Santiam Kalapuya lands, including hundreds of thousands of acres, to the US government.[5]

Three weeks later, Chief Coast-no of the Santiam Band of Molallas signed a similar treaty to establish a reservation for his people that included some of their ancestral lands of the upper North Santiam canyon (it appears that the North Fork canyon may have been included in this reservation, but the maps are not detailed enough to be clear). Officials sent these and four other treaties signed with Willamette Valley tribes to Washington, DC, for ratification. However, by the time Congress considered the treaties, American settlers had claimed these areas of rich farmland—some of the finest in Oregon—and congressional leaders knew there would be more conflicts if those newest settlers were told to leave. As a result, the treaties were thrown out.[6]

Four years later, the superintendent of Indian Affairs for the Oregon Territory drafted a new treaty for all the Native people of the Willamette Valley including the Kalapuyans and Molallans, along with others at and near Willamette Falls, but this version was far less favorable to the tribal communities. The draft asserted that more than 7 million acres of land, including the entire Willamette Valley, would be ceded to the US government, including the North Fork and all lands of the Santiam watershed. All tribes and bands living on these lands, including the Santiam Band of Kalapuyas and the Santiam Band of Molallas, would be sent to one reservation, the size and location to be determined. Called the "Treaty with the Kalapuya, Etc.," also known as the Kalapuya Treaty or the Willamette Valley Treaty, it was signed on January 22, 1855, and ratified in Washington, DC, five weeks later, but without a reservation having been established yet, Native people immediately found themselves with no homes or land and nowhere to go.[7] In some cases, Native people went to work for the settlers within the Willamette Valley, who provided them a temporary place to live.[8]

Ten months after the Willamette Valley Treaty was signed, US President Franklin Pierce finally issued an executive order to establish a permanent reservation. Called the Coast Reservation, it included lands along Oregon's Pacific coast and was intended for tribal members from across western Oregon. Shortly thereafter, President James Buchanan signed an additional order to create the Grand Ronde Reservation along the Yamhill River, 30 miles west of Salem, in fulfillment of the 1855 Willamette Valley Treaty.[9]

Tribal members from throughout western Oregon were forced by US authorities to relocate to their designated reservations, and many were forced to travel on foot. Allowed to take only what they could carry, they had to leave most of their possessions behind. Some were forced to walk long distances in winter weather and over rough terrain. An observer, Lieutenant E. O. C. Ord, witnessed one of the removals of people from their land. He recalled, "Left behind were the bones of parents, grandparents, and ancestors, ages-old villages and fisheries, and a way of life well-tuned to the rhythms of a beautiful land." Leaving their homelands, these journeys are still referred to by tribal members as the Trails of Tears.[10]

Those who went to the Coast Reservation came to be members of the Confederated Tribes of Siletz Indians, while those who relocated to the Grand Ronde Reservation came to be known as members of the Confederated Tribes of Grand Ronde Community of Oregon.[11]

Making the transition to reservation life was extremely difficult. People came from many tribes and spoke different languages and lived according to different traditions. The Native people were expected to farm, but reservation soils were of marginal quality and the new residents did not come with farming experience. They did not receive all the provisions promised in the treaties, such as tools and training. They were largely prohibited from owning guns, so they could not hunt, and in most cases they were not allowed to leave the reservation unless they had permission from local Indian agents who worked for the US government. With few exceptions, Native children were required to attend boarding schools away from home, where they were forbidden to speak their own languages or practice their customs. With limited food supplies and inadequate housing on the reservations, more people died.[12]

In spite of these wide-ranging challenges, Native people persevered. Some went to work for logging companies while others took jobs on farms. The Hudson family at Grand Ronde, descendants of Chief Alquema, among others, continued their tradition of basket-making, sometimes making and selling specially designed baskets with handles to American settlers.[13]

After several years researching Native history, including the removal of Native people to reservations, I became aware there was still yet more to learn about the story. Inconceivably, after facing years of hardship on the reservations, the Western Oregon Indian Termination Act of 1954 cancelled all US obligations to the Siletz and Grand Ronde tribes outlined in their treaties. As a result, western Oregon's Native people lost all benefits guaranteed through the treaties and lost their legal status as American Indians. The Siletz and Grand Ronde reservations closed, and their lands were sold by the US government. At Siletz, their tribal cemetery was transferred to the city of Siletz to be used as a park. According to the Bureau of Indian Affairs, each tribal member at Siletz was paid $542.50 compensation. At Grand Ronde, tribal members were paid an average of $35 each.[14] At Grand Ronde, although now they were virtually landless, the tribe was allowed to retain the tribal cemetery.[15]

By the early 1970s, determined Native people from both Siletz and Grand Ronde began advocating for restoration of their lands and tribal rights. Congress took up the matter and held hearings. A sixteen-year-old tribal member spoke during congressional hearings:

> All my life, I have only known termination. People ask me what tribe I am, and when I tell them, they've never heard of it. That in itself would mean a lot to me: for people to know that I am part of the Molalla Tribe of the Grand Rondes, and how proud I am to be a member of my tribe.[16]

Through the strength and resiliency of Native people, Congress restored the Confederated Tribes of Siletz Indians in 1977 and the Confederated Tribes of Grand Ronde in 1983. A small amount of land was returned to the tribes, and some tribal rights were restored. Overcoming unimaginable hardships, tribal members at both Siletz and Grand Ronde have endured, continuing to practice their rich traditions and sharing them today. Each year on the anniversary of their respective restorations, both tribal nations celebrate with powwows and other special events.

During the years of my research, I got to know tribal member Stephanie Craig at Grand Ronde. A traditional Kalapuya basket-weaver and descendant of the Hudson family, Stephanie shared stories with me

The Hudson family at Grand Ronde, c. 1900. (*Photo courtesy of Oregon Historical Society, Portland, Oregon.*)

numerous times. While talking with her at the Chachalu Museum and Cultural Center at Grand Ronde one day, she showed me a basket in the museum collection dating back to the time before European and American immigrants came to the Pacific Northwest. She asked if I would like to hold it; when I hesitated, she insisted, "This is a living basket, meant to be held and used, not simply to be viewed inside a glass case."

As I carefully held the intricately woven basket, I thought about how far my learning had come. Just a few years earlier, I knew nothing of the Kalapuyan or Molallan people. Now I was sitting in the archive room of the Confederated Tribes of Grand Ronde, learning Oregon's Native history from tribal members as I held a cherished part of tribal culture and history in my hands. I had not only learned about a rich Native history along the North Fork reaching back thousands of years, I had also met and formed relationships within a resilient Native culture alive and thriving in Oregon today.

6
The Gateway

I thought a good place to start learning about American settlement of the North Fork was at the very mouth of the river in the historic town of Mehama. Luckily, a friend had lived in the tiny community for many years and suggested we gather several other longtime residents for a group conversation.

The following week, five proudly self-described "old-timers" joined me for coffee at the Gingerbread House Restaurant, a popular local burger spot. We ordered coffee and got acquainted. Our conversation began easily as we glanced up at the black-and-white photos of the original Gingerbread House on the wall just above our table. We all remembered the place from the 1950s, when it was new and we were all young. I told the group my family often stopped there for ice cream on our way home from the cabin, and they shared their own memories, such as ordering the Gingerbread Special with ice cream.

One man mentioned a document he thought would be helpful in understanding the history of Mehama—a diary of one of the first families to settle in the area, the Stouts. A few weeks later, I found the Stout diary at the Oregon Historical Society in Portland. It was a real find.

The diary told of twenty-three-year-old Lewis Stout, who traveled the Oregon Trail by wagon from Iowa in 1852 alongside his parents in a second wagon. Theirs is much like other stories of western migration. Traveling for six months as part of a wagon train with other families, they covered nearly 2,000 miles, averaging about 10 miles a day. The diary tells how they drove through vast herds of bison, had many contacts with Native people, lost a wagon in the Platte River, and nearly lost everything else when a brush fire swept over their camp only days from their destination. They passed countless graves of other immigrants along the trail, testament to the perils of that cross-continental journey. Once in Oregon,

The town of Smith's Ferry, later named Mehama, c. 1890, looking west with the main stem North Santiam River in the distance. On the left is Smith Hotel, adjacent to the boardwalks that lined the muddy streets in winter. On the right, saddled horses are seen in the large livery stable, a place where visitors could temporarily board their horses. (*Photograph by Andrew and Louis Siegmund. Courtesy of Oregon State Library and Lou Siegmund, a descendant.*)

the Stouts filed homestead claims about a mile from where the Little North Santiam enters the main North Santiam at what is now Mehama. For the first few years, they were among the few settlers in the area.[1]

By 1857, the Stouts had built a sawmill specializing in cedar lumber along a small creek, the first known sawmill in Santiam country. It generated power from a small creek, and much of the lumber was delivered 25 miles to Salem by horse-drawn wagon. Lewis and some neighbors established a ferry to service travelers and community members across the North Santiam River. Constructed with lumber from the mill, the ferry was kept on course by a fiber rope stretched across the river and was ingeniously powered by the river current.[2]

Within a few years, another new arrival, James X. Smith, took over the operation. The ferry—and the town that sprang up on the north side of the river—took on the name Smith's Ferry. Smith and his wife also established the Smith Hotel. During the town's early years, residents reported seeing Native people pass through along the main North Santiam River. Some were likely Kalapuyans who still came up the canyon to dig camas, while others likely included Molallans, as well as people from the Klamath, Wasco, and Warm Springs tribes who came from east of the mountains to trade in the Willamette Valley.[3]

With more and more people coming to the area, the town of Smith's Ferry grew quickly. The first school opened in 1866, and its first Sunday school met in the school, as there was not yet a church building. In 1877, Smith's Ferry became the first registered town along the North Santiam River. James Smith took advantage of the establishment of a post office to rename the town after his wife Mehama.[4]

As I continued to follow leads from the Gingerbread House old-timers, I found more stories and early photographs; the town's history continued to unfold for me. A blacksmith shop and a general store opened. Two grist mills opened near town. Local farmers brought grain to the mills to be ground into flour, and the millers were known to accept some of the grain as payment. A bridge constructed across the North Santiam in 1887 ended ferry operations.

At about that time, Methodists constructed the first church in Mehama. Presbyterians followed, building a sizable church using land and building materials donated by the Smiths.[5] Worshipers at the new church kept warm on cold mornings around a large round wood-burning stove and sang hymns accompanied by a pump organ while light entered the church through colored windows.[6]

Descriptions of this church remind me of the Spring Valley Church in the countryside northwest of Salem I attended as a boy. It was also built by Presbyterians in the 1800s, though it had no colored windows. One of our church-goers at Spring Valley, Mr. Denny, regularly drove out to the church early on cold Sunday mornings to start a fire in the wood-burning stove so the building would be warm when worshippers arrived. Everyone stood close around that stove on cold Sunday mornings, hoping the hard wooden pews might warm up just a little bit more before taking our seats. I expect the Mehama Presbyterian Church also had a person like Mr. Denny who looked out for the comfort of fellow church-goers.

By 1899, worshipers at the Mehama Presbyterian church decided to add a bell to the steeple, so they placed an order for one to be cast in Ohio and shipped to Oregon. Community members hung it in the bell tower, where it announced Sunday services and other special gatherings.[7] My new friends at the Gingerbread House also described how the church was built with hand tools and square nails. It stood for nearly sixty years, a landmark in this small town. By 1953, it had fallen into disrepair and was demolished.[8] The Mehama Community Church occupies the site today.

Shortly after I'd learned about the town's early churches, I called Troy Gulstrom, pastor at the Mehama Community Church, to ask whether the bell hanging in the current church might be the original bell from the old Presbyterian Church. He said people thought it was, but there was no documentation to confirm it. We both wanted to know for sure and agreed the only way to find out would be to climb into the bell tower and see if it had a date stamped on it, something that old bells often have.

The day came and we both started climbing toward the bell—first up some stairs, then a ladder, and finally into the exposed interior framing of the bell tower. The way was tight and dark. Having a slender build like my dad's, I was elected to finish the climb on my own, using my camping headlamp to find my way. When I finally reached the huge bell, I could only twist myself around to view it from one side—and there were no visible markings there. My only other option was to reach around behind it with the camera on my phone and photograph the hidden side of the bell. Maybe I could find something in a photo. The first photo: blurred. The second: nothing. On the third photo, I could read a date stamped in the bell. I yelled down through the tower.

"Troy, I found a date. It reads 12-13-99."

It was the original bell from 1899. Climbing back down and dusting myself off, I looked at Troy. He was smiling. It was like we just won the million-dollar lottery.

"You wanna ring it?" he offered with a wide grin.

It took a couple of pulls on the thick rope to get the bell swaying, but by the third pull, it began to ring—a deep resonant sound that vibrated through the church. I smiled back and told him it reminded me of helping my dad ring the bell at the Spring Valley Church when I was a boy.

By 1879, the town of Mehama had its general store that later also served as the post office, drug store, and just about everything else. Owned by Civil War veteran and Michigan immigrant Dr. Rollin Pratt, for many years the store had a sign out front that read, "Drugstore Books & Stationary & Amunition." According to the personal writings of Ray Stout (Lewis Stout's youngest son, who grew up in Mehama), no one seemed concerned about the wrong spelling of the word ammunition.

Dr. Pratt served as physician, druggist, storekeeper, and postmaster. Traveling by horse and buggy, he made house calls and sometimes performed surgeries without hospital facilities. Inside the store, Dr. Pratt's potbelly stove kept the place warm and provided a gathering place for townspeople during cold or rainy weather.

By the late 1880s, a daily stagecoach ran the 17 miles between Mehama and the town of Turner near Salem. It left Mehama at 6 a.m., met the eleven o'clock train at Turner, and then returned to Mehama by dinner time. The return of the daily coach became a community event

Mehama-Turner stage in front of the Smith Hotel, c. 1900. This is the only known photo of the stage that provided transportation between Mehama and the Willamette Valley for many years. It is said that Mehama Smith often sat by the hotel windows to wave at passersby and welcome them to town. (*Photo courtesy of Willamette Heritage Center, Salem, Oregon.*)

because it carried everything from people to supplies, and the mail. When the stage was late—as it often was—people gathered around the woodstove to wait, tell stories, and catch up on news.[9]

For more than three decades, the Smith Hotel served residents, miners, and summer vacationers from Salem and other Willamette Valley towns. The hotel often filled to capacity, and the overflow was accommodated in nearby homes.

The hotel became well known throughout the Willamette Valley, and it was said that "Aunt Mehama" was a charming hostess. According to a news article, her meals were "the finest in the land." She was known to personally welcome everyone who came to the hotel and make them feel at home. Salem's *Capital Journal* newspaper in 1885 carried a story stating that the hotel had become "a charming mountain resort entertaining the traveler, trout fisher, summer tourist, sportsman and wheelman."

Even as she ran the hotel, Mehama devoted herself to community affairs, serving as superintendent of the Mehama School, postmistress of the Mehama Post Office, and superintendent of the Sunday school. When she passed away in 1895, memorial services held at the hotel were attended by many. Her body was taken to Salem in a horse-drawn wagon for burial, a 25-mile trip that took six hours.[10] James Smith lived for sixteen more years. The Smiths are buried side by side in the Pioneer Cemetery near my home in southeast Salem, where I often walk. Seeing their weather-worn gravestones draws me back to their story, connecting me more closely to the early days of Mehama.

One day I found a Ray Stout poem titled "Waiting for the Mail." It recalled the small town of Mehama in the 1880s and 1890s, the woodstove in Pratt's store, and the importance of the stage to the community.[11] I especially like the closing lines:

Ah, me, those days I can't forget,
Where once I lived of yore,
And in that same old smoke-filled room,
I would like to be once more.
Amid old friends and neighbors,
And hear again the tale,
Of all the brave and daring deeds,
While waiting for the mail

Like Ray Stout, I often think with fondness on experiences, people, and places from my youth. It's not hard for me to understand how Ray would have liked to go back to experience those earlier years of his life in the small town he loved so much.

Through its early years, everyone heading east into the mountains, including Native people who still walked the old trails, passed through the town that grew into a bustling mountain resort destination.

Thank goodness we have people who remember their local history. I appreciate my new friends—that group of Mehama "old-timers" that pointed me toward an appreciation for the stories of this small Oregon town that became the gateway to the North Fork.

7
Seeking Gold

While working for the Forest Service in Idaho, I lived in the Sawtooth Valley east of Boise, an area filled with rich mining and homesteading history dating from the 1870s and 1880s. My ranger-boss was a descendant of Sawtooth Valley homesteaders, and one of the nearby peaks was named for his grandfather. Our small community of about twenty full-time residents stood near the ruins of the original Sawtooth City boom town that still echoed with mining stories from decades past. Located in the Sawtooth National Forest, the area's mining history was widely known, thanks to interpretive signs, brochures, and guidebooks presented by the Forest Service and local writers.

By contrast, I knew there must be information about the early North Fork mines tucked away in books and museums, but through the years, I'd heard very little about these parts of canyon history. All that began to change one day when historian Dr. Bob Reinhardt sparked my interest in a prospector's journal from the North Fork written in the 1860s that had been sitting at our own Oregon Historical Society in Portland.

The journal turned out to be 37 pages of pure gold for me. The stories in that well-preserved old leather-bound journal became one of the special finds of my research journey.

According to the journal, on July 6, 1864, seven men entered the North Fork on horseback for a weeklong trip to look for gold in the upper canyon. They had passed the community of Smith's Ferry as they approached the mountains. The writer—who never identifies himself—described following an old Indian trail, elk trails, and more recent miner and hunter trails. He also described the rugged landscape that few non-Native people

Facing page: Mining Camp at Jawbone Flats, c. 1930s. In mid-winter, the small mining community often endured heavy accumulations of snow, making travel difficult and hazardous. Battle Ax Creek, a tributary of the Little North Santiam, can be seen in the lower left corner. (*Photo courtesy of Tom Atiyeh and Opal Creek Ancient Forest Center.*)

had yet seen. Little is known about these men except from what appears in this soft leather-bound journal. Written in pencil, the text mentions only a few place-names, likely because few geographic features had been named by westerners at that time.

The writer chronicled their arduous journey. When fording the river on the first day, one of the horses slipped, sending both animal and rider plunging into deep water—not a good start. At a location near present-day Elkhorn, the route became too difficult for the horses, so one man stayed behind with the animals while the others continued up the canyon on foot. Each man carried a pack with basic provisions: a blanket, a tin cup, fishing line, bread, cheese, bacon, and beans. The writer also carried an ax, and others likely carried prospecting tools such as picks, shovels, and gold-mining pans.

At a treacherous stretch of river, the men cut two trees and fashioned a bridge that allowed them to cross over by sliding in a sitting position. In another place they leapt across a chasm from a high point on one side to a tall rock on the other. All made it safely, although one man landed with a jolt and lost his hat into the swirling water, which reportedly led to heckling from his comrades.

Along the way they drank spring water that the writer describes as "the best and coldest water we ever tasted." They caught trout and ate a lot of "whortle berries" (a European term for blueberries). The fresh trout and sweet berries must have been a welcome change from the salty, starchy food they carried. The journal reports that one man ate so many wild berries he got sick.

The writer took time to describe the landscape as they made their way up the remote canyon.

> On some of the highest points we stop to look over the country around, most grand and sublime in the scenery. On our right and left high and rugged mountains are seen in the distance while almost beneath our feet at frightful depth rolls there the river of the Santiam through kasams and falls and rocks overhanging its winding way of stupendous magnitude. A panorama of nature's grandeur, scenery is here spread before us. I doubt whether human eyes ever beheld its like before. (July 7, 1864)

At one point the group found itself in a nearly impossible spot and discussed how to proceed. They decided to cross the ice-cold stream and climbed a nearly vertical rock wall. Two hundred feet above the water, the writer slipped. He wrote, "I hung suspended for a moment high in the air—on the verge of eternity." They remained calm and managed to reach the top of the cliff and continued up-canyon.

The writer described the mountains as "covered with an immense growth of fir, hemlock and cedar of the most beautiful kind. On the crest, . . . pine of a stunted growth and mountain laurel now in full bloom, the blossoms very fragrant and beautiful. Its beauty would surpass any of the most beautiful flowers in the City of Salem."

By the third day, the group arrived at a promising site called Henline Camp on Fall Creek but found that it had already been claimed by other miners, forcing them to move on up the canyon to find other places to prospect. For two more days they examined rocks and looked for gold, finally staking several claims by posting them with written notices.

Fatigued, and with provisions running low, they made their way out of the upper canyon, finally returning to their colleagues and horses awaiting mid-canyon. It had been a difficult trip. The final entry in the journal reads: "No limbs broken, satisfied to escape from those wild and solitary regions."[1]

Paging through the old journal, I was transported to the North Fork in the 1800s, to the rugged and wild landscape Native people had known for thousands of years. The journal inspired in me a desire for a deeper look, and I began poring over files at the Canyon Life Museum in Mill City for more information on the canyon's mining era.

Exploring the upper North Fork canyon when we were young, my friends and I sometimes came upon evidence of the mining era: dilapidated mine shafts in the mountainsides, rusting mining equipment, and long steel cables stretching through the forest. I admired the creativity and ingenuity needed to get large steel equipment into narrow ravines and onto steep mountainsides. One day we discovered an abandoned log cabin not far from one of the mine shafts. Leaning a bit but still solid, its log walls and wood-shingled roof led me to wonder what life must have been like for the people who built it in such a remote and wild location. Even in my teens, I knew that their work had to have been challenging and exhausting—and dangerous. Now I began to learn their stories.

The Civil War came to a close in the late 1860s, releasing countless men to fill the upper canyon as prospectors and miners. Many probably came because local news reports of that time proclaimed the tremendous mineral potential in the area. One article read, "Thousands of millions of tons of ore are under the Eternal Hills up there."[2] Another story quoted an old California miner: "If I were a younger man, I would be willing to stake my all in the Santiam mines. The specimens show that the Santiam region is very similar to some of the richest auriferous districts in California."[3]

Among the early prospectors to enter the upper canyon, brothers Francis and William Henline established a claim along Fall Creek in 1860 (this would have been the "Henline Camp" claim mentioned in the prospector's journal). It was the first formally registered claim in the area, and they named it Silver King Mine. Fall Creek is now known as Henline Creek, which is on the south flank of Henline Mountain. The waterfall at the mine site and the rugged glacier-carved mountain rising above it are also named for these hearty miners.[4]

Near the base of Henline Falls, miners excavated their main tunnel a third of a mile into solid rock. A penstock (pipe) brought water down from above the falls into a water wheel near the tunnel entrance to generate power for the mine. A nearby blacksmith shop, bunkhouse, and cookhouse supported the operation.

Through the years, my family and I have walked many times along what I now know to be the old miner's trail to view the 126-foot Henline Falls. We often peered into the dark dripping mine shaft next to the falls and studied the nearby cement foundations, wondering about the history of the place. Today, all the old structures have long since vanished, but the cement base from the water wheel remains. Since learning about the Silver King, we've returned to the falls with new knowledge of the mine's history and marvel at the stories of the intrepid miners who came there in search of silver and gold more than 150 years earlier.

Soon after the Silver King got started, more mines opened, among them the Black Eagle Mine, just west of Gold Creek. Like at Silver King, miners made extensive developments: a sawmill, power plant, bunkhouses, and a small mill for concentrating ore.[5]

Working at the mines was risky business. A man fell to his death while working on the cliffs high above the Silver King. A dynamite explosion seriously hurt two brothers, and one died while working at the Black Eagle.[6]

By the late 1880s, a rail line along the main North Santiam River made traveling up the North Fork easier and faster.[7] Miners could now ride the rails to Gatesville, transfer their heavy supplies from train cars to pack animals, and follow a trail over Gates Hill into the North Fork mines. The Gates Hill route was nearly 8 miles shorter than the route up the North Fork from Mehama and was later widened to accommodate wagon traffic. Gatesville became a boom town, serving as the nearest supply depot for the North Fork mines. Residents eventually shortened the name to Gates.[8]

Heavily loaded wagons using the new Gates Hill Road needed good brakes for the steep descent into Elkhorn Valley. Teamsters often stopped at the crest and cut several trees to drag behind their wagons to serve as extra brakes on the way down. Old-timers reported large piles of logs at the bottom of the road thrown aside after each descent.

Miners at the Black Eagle Mine, c. 1900. The men appear ready to enter the mine to begin their shift with picks and candles in hand. Each candle was mounted in a metal holder that could be wedged into a crack in the rock or hung on wood timbers to enable hands-free work. Several candles were needed to illuminate even a small work area. (*Photo courtesy of North Santiam Historical Society, Mill City, Oregon.*)

North Fork canyon and miner's cabin at the Black Eagle Mine, c. 1900, showing the rugged upper canyon and a mix of living and burnt trees, evidence of a recent forest fire. A foot trail ascended the mountainside in the lower right corner of the photo. (*Photo courtesy of North Santiam Historical Society, Mill City, Oregon.*)

Through the years that followed, miners dug and blasted more than two hundred horizontal mine tunnels in the area, yet most North Fork mines had closed or were listed for sale by the mid-1920s. It might have looked like the end of mining in the canyon, but Portland entrepreneur James Hewitt saw an opportunity. He established the Amalgamated Mining Company, staked some claims, and pulled together investors to purchase some of the already established mines in the most remote part of the canyon, determined he could be the one to hit the elusive vein of gold.[9]

Improving the road to his mines presented a major hurdle for the new owner. Some mountainsides were solid rock cliffs. His team engineered a creative solution that avoided major blasting: dynamiting just enough rock to form half the road width, and then building "half-bridges" to form the outer half of the road. The unusual bridges became a unique element of the area's character that I crossed many times over the years.

By 1934, miners had built their main camp at a site that came to be known as Jawbone Flats. They constructed cabins and bunkhouses, a cookhouse, and a commissary plus three mills for processing rock from the mines. Jawbone became a fully functional community, with a water-powered generator producing electricity for lights and tools.

Hewitt constructed a sawmill nearby to produce lumber for the mines, but when two log trucks slid off the narrow mining road and tumbled into the canyon, lumber operations were done. The Amalgamated Mines operated until the early 1940s but closed with the coming of World War II. It was the last major mining venture along the North Fork.[10]

One of the few mining-era stories I heard as a boy, but never could believe, was a gruesome story about a man who walked out from the mines in deep snow one winter and nearly died. Recently I heard the story again, yet still held it back as a tall tale. But as I dug deeper, I came upon an obituary of a man named James Church. This was the story I'd heard years ago—and it was true! I soon learned there was a lot more to the story than what I'd heard.

Born in Canada in 1853, James Church came to the North Fork at age twenty-seven. He staked a mining claim in the upper canyon, homesteaded in Elkhorn Valley, built a cabin there and began operating a pack string of mules to carry supplies up-canyon to the mines. In later years, he hauled supplies by mule-drawn wagon.

In December of 1884, this robust packer made a trip to the mines with his dog and another miner. They had no way to know that the epic Oregon winter storm of 1884 was brewing. The weather turned bitterly cold, with heavy snow, and they ran out of food. They waited for a pause in the weather but finally decided to make a break for it on foot, along with Church's dog. The snow was deep and travel by foot was slow, so they took refuge at a deserted mining camp along the way. Desperately cold and hungry, they killed the dog for food. After several days of rest and no letup in the storm, they agreed James would continue on to his home in Elkhorn Valley while his companion stayed back. Wrapping his feet in the skin of the dog, Church set out through snow that was now 5 feet deep in places.

Struggling, sometimes crawling, he made it to Elkhorn Valley. He arrived in the evening at a home where people were gathered for a dance

Local packers at Gates ready for a trip into the mountains along narrow trails, c. late 1800s. Construction of wagon roads later allowed mule-drawn wagons to carry supplies to the mines. (*Photo courtesy of North Santiam Historical Society, Mill City, Oregon.*)

and was given aid. Friends and neighbors took him in and organized a group to rescue his friend. James's legs were so badly frostbitten that by the time a doctor arrived, they could not be saved. With no anesthetic available—according to local lore—he took a bottle of whiskey to dull the pain. The doctor drew a hand saw from his black bag and amputated both legs just below the knees. The rescue party successfully brought out the second miner, who also lost his legs to frostbite. Both men survived the tragic experience and left the area for a time.

After recovering from his ordeal, Church returned to his home on the North Fork with an adapted Studebaker freight wagon and resumed hauling supplies to the North Fork mines with a team of mules. He had a short post installed in the middle of his seat (like the horn on a saddle) to help him stay in place when roads got rough. He walked with crutches or sometimes walked on the stumps of his legs. He had a special platform built at his home in Elkhorn Valley from which he harnessed animals and loaded wagons.

He regularly picked up freight—and sometimes passengers—at the Gates train depot before making his run over the steep Gates Hill. Near the depot, he had a stable where he had another loading platform built. He was known to have a loud voice and people said that from Gates you could hear him calling—sometimes cursing at—his mules as they strained up Gates Hill. He is said to have often locked the rear wheels of the freight wagon and raced down the mountainside into Elkhorn Valley, likely to the alarm of his passengers.

Church built cabins and bridges, served as a guide throughout the mountains, and was known as a great entertainer. A Salem newspaper account in 1904 stated, "To see Church hook up his mules and get around sets at defiance all previous conceptions of human limitations." When he died in 1909 at age fifty-eight, reports suggest that, upon Church's request, the minister broke a bottle of whiskey over his grave. He is buried in the Fox Valley Cemetery just east of Lyons.[11]

Despite the fact that mining in the canyon was difficult, risky, and deadly for some, North Fork miners showed remarkable strength and courage in entering this rugged country, packing heavy equipment, developing mining operations, and enduring the challenges of life in the wilds. No one displayed the ability to respond to these challenges with determination and resilience better than the legendary Canadian, James Church.

For all the excitement and hopes for major profits, only small amounts of gold, silver, copper, lead, and zinc were ever taken from any of the North Fork mines. Much of the physical evidence of the mining ventures in the North Fork canyon is gone, and it has often been said that more money was invested in the mines than was ever generated by them.

Death of James Church.

James Church, an old-time teamster, at Gates, died this week at the age of about 58 years. Years ago he had both feet frozen off, but continued to do team work, at one time running a six mule team into the mines, getting around on a shoe fitted to his knees He had been married but years ago separated from his wife.

James Church obituary from the *Albany Democrat* newspaper, June 18, 1909. (*Image courtesy of Lee Enterprises, Omaha, Nebraska.*)

8
Newcomers

At the same time as miners explored up the canyon with dreams of striking gold, other newcomers ventured up the river in search of a different kind of treasure: favorable homesites. Even some of the miners like James Church couldn't pass up the opportunity to claim a homestead in Elkhorn Valley.

Along the lower stretch of the river, I had known of the place called Taylor's Grove all my life—we passed it each time on the way to Elkhorn—but I did not know of the people named Taylor who lived there nor the story of the place we always knew as "The Grove." In recent years, I picked up information about early settlers Marion and Martha Taylor from interviews with longtime residents and from news articles: their love for the North Fork, its healing power, and the couple's desire to share its health benefits with others.

Marion's parents had come west with a wagon train on the Oregon Trail in 1844 and homesteaded in the hills between Salem and Smith's Ferry. Their son Marion was born four years later. Martha was born on the Great Plains while her parents traveled with another wagon train. Tragically, her mother died en route, and baby Martha completed the journey with her father.

Both raised in Oregon, Marion and Martha married in 1871, but at just twenty-three years old Marion became ill and was given only six months to live. Doctors advised him to spend more time outdoors and suggested he eat lots of venison to restore his health. With this prescription, Marion and Martha set out to have a home built along the North Fork, two miles east of Smith's Ferry. Marion was so ill he needed to be carried into their new home on a stretcher.

Facing page: Martha and Marion Taylor, c. 1930. (*Photo courtesy of North Santiam Historical Society, Mill City, Oregon.*)

The outdoor therapy paid off. Marion's health improved in only a few months, and he claimed to be the "livest" person in the county. He attributed his recovery to the clean air, forests, streams, and beauty of the Cascade mountains, and he wanted to share the health benefits with others. He and Martha turned part of their property into a rustic resort for recreation and relaxation, where people could come to picnic, fish, camp, and be renewed by the outdoors.

A newspaper article from the time described Taylor's Grove:

> A well-known campground on the Little North Fork of the Santiam River, for years a source of pleasure for people who enjoy fishing and a trip into the mountains, [it offers] clean shady grounds and a wonderful spring of pure cold water. Taylor's Grove is one of the most noted and best appreciated mountain resorts in the area.

Years later Marion said, "My faith in the health-giving resources of the Cascades has never wavered. When our friends in the valley were ailing and losing their spirit and their 'pep,' we invited them up to the hills, to 'come back' and recuperate. That's how we came to establish 'the grove' for those who need a spell in the outdoors." [1]

This story reminded me of our family's early years at Elkhorn—some fifty years after Marion Taylor made his statement—when going up the North Fork seemed to us like going to a mountain retreat. Even though my dad likely never heard Marion Taylor's quote, he used to say his time up the river was "nature therapy," a world away from deadlines and stresses of his labor in a noisy printshop. Time along this beautiful stream has offered me the same rest and rejuvenation that Marion and my dad spoke of, when rest and healing have been critically important for my own health. The towering mountains, the clear rushing water, the changing seasons and, most recently, the return of life to the burned forest, continually refresh and lift my spirits. Both Marion and Martha lived into their nineties. Long after their beloved resort closed, a large sign still identified the area as Taylor's Grove.

Even before the Taylors settled there, explorers and settlers had often crossed the river at this site; it was located along a well-used historic travel route called the Minto Trail (it has been speculated by some historians that the Minto Trail was actually the Klamath-Molalla Trail. If that is true, this river crossing may have been used by Native people for thousands of years).[2] In time, a covered bridge was built that improved travel through the area and linked Taylor's Grove with other developments across the river. The bridge was eventually named the Marion Taylor Bridge in honor of the early settler.[3]

Across the river from Taylor's Grove stood the one-room Oakdale School, another feature that my family passed on the way to Elkhorn. Norma Pennington, a spry ninety-year-old, had been a student there in the 1930s and shared her memories of the school when I visited with her in 2017.

Norma told me the school was established in 1878 and that students in grades 1–8 from the lower North Fork canyon gathered around a woodstove for warmth on cold mornings and played in the oak grove and surrounding meadow during recess. One teacher taught all grades for up to fifteen students. The schoolhouse also served as a community hall, hosting many social events until it closed in the 1940s. Over the years, the building fell into disrepair. Although we could tell it was being used as a barn, years later the old sign above the front doors still read "Oakdale School."[4]

Intrigued by the old school, one day I asked permission from the property owner to take a look inside. Walking toward the schoolhouse, I noticed blue camas flowers growing in the meadow nearby. Since the front steps were missing, I entered the building from the back and stepped into the main room, now filled with bales of hay. There was no longer a woodstove, but I could see where its pipe once penetrated the ceiling and could imagine kids warming their hands next to the radiant heat. Just inside the front door I found walk-in closets with rows of hooks where kids likely hung their coats at the start of the school day.

As I stepped over to a window and looked out through the old-style wavy glass at the oaks that gave the school its name, I recalled talking with Bill Hueller, a man whose grandparents and parents had owned the property many years before. He told me the earliest settlers reported the oak grove had been a meeting place for Indians, and that they had found arrow points and other evidence of Native people there. He said an old Indian trail passed through the area and that the trail was where the road is now.[5] I lingered at the window as cars streaked by on North Fork Road, and I thought about the meadow, the oaks, and the many people who had come there across time.

By 1890, homesteaders upriver from Taylor's Grove began to settle in Elkhorn Valley. Records offer glowing accounts of the abundance of game there, including a story told by Minnie McCarty, a descendant of area homesteaders. Life on the North Fork was not easy, but Minnie's story reveals that the abundant elk that gave Elkhorn its name provided a steady economy for the homesteaders.

"The Elkhorn District well deserved its name," she explained, then continued:

> Each fall the early settlers [along the main North Santiam River] went there [to Elkhorn Valley] for their winter supply of meat. They cut up and dried or smoked the meat at the hunting grounds and brought home both meat and hides. It was a large part of both their cash and barter economy, since meat and hides could be sold or traded for staple groceries and supplies in Albany, Salem, or Portland.

Residents tanned the hides and the women made gloves to sell in Willamette Valley markets. The cash was highly valued in the rural economy.[6] Since bull elk shed their antlers each year, many sets of antlers (sometimes incorrectly called "elk horns") would have been scattered across this flat area along the North Fork. Minnie's story offers the best account I've found of the likely origin of the name Elkhorn Valley. Similarly, a Bureau of Land Management cultural resource document suggests the Elkhorn area may have been named for "the many elk that once wintered in the valley."[7]

Among the early settlers I learned about were Robert and Lena Morehouse. Their log home in Elkhorn Valley may have been located along Morehouse Creek, which flows near the base of Gates Hill Road and through the present-day Elkhorn Valley Golf Course.

The Morehouse children would have attended the Elkhorn school, 10 miles upriver from Oakdale. It was also a one-room building, warmed by a woodstove and nearly identical in design to the Oakdale school. I'd never known of this school and didn't remember ever seeing it in Elkhorn Valley, yet I now understand what a valuable part of life it was, allowing families to live in this remote area and still provide children with a formal education.

The Morehouse family at their home in Elkhorn Valley, c. 1890. The elk antlers offer evidence of the elk that roamed the canyon in those years. Photograph by Andrew and Louis Siegmund. (*Photo courtesy of Oregon State Library and Lou Siegmund, a descendant.*)

In the midst of my research, I picked up an exuberant phone call from a friend at the Canyon Life Museum who told me that Carl Pope, a descendant of early Elkhorn homesteaders, had stopped by the museum looking for information on his family's history, and that he would like to speak with me. I was excited to hear that Carl had stories about Temple (Tel) and Jennie May Pope, his grandparents, who homesteaded in Elkhorn in the early 1890s.

Carl told me his grandparents had built a log cabin and barn and planted an orchard. Because the best soil was across the North Fork from their house, they built a swinging bridge over the river to access their garden. Stories from the time indicate the garden was so productive, family members carried huge potatoes over the bridge to the house like armloads of firewood.

The Elkhorn Post Office was established on the Pope property in 1892, and Jennie May became postmistress. The Post Office operated there until 1917, when fire destroyed it. After the fire, postal services moved to Gates, with no further mail delivery to Elkhorn.[8]

With construction of the wagon road over Gates Hill, a lot of new activity stirred in the Elkhorn Valley. As more and more miners passed through, the Popes transformed their Elkhorn homestead into a pack station. Tel kept supplies and a string of mules to accommodate explorers and miners, while Jennie Mae cooked meals for the guests, needing only a few basic ingredients to produce outstanding meals. At the pack station, miners transferred supplies from freight wagons to pack animals for completing the journey into the mines up the narrow canyon trail.

Before I met Norma Pennington, I already knew she held a deep interest in Santiam country history, but I hadn't realized her depth of knowledge and interest in the North Fork. I also didn't know she held keen research skills. In her soft, high-pitched voice, she told me she had grown up in the Mehama area and lived at a nearby sawmill called the Crabtree Mill, where her father worked. I was delighted when she offered to search newspaper archives for me and turned up a North Fork mining and homesteading story from Salem's *Daily Capital Journal* dated June 28, 1904.

The article said a team of county officials had embarked on a trip up the North Fork to explore the potential for a new section of wagon road from Elkhorn to the mines. The writer accompanied the group and described traveling by train from Salem through Albany and up to Gates. They were taken by freight wagon over Gates Hill by James Church, reaching the end of the wagon road at Elkhorn by eight o'clock, in time for a late supper. The group split into two, one staying at the Pope ranch, the other group staying at a nearby ranch belonging to Perry and Olive Darling (what I wouldn't give to ask them what it was like to ride over Gates Hill with James Church!). It's not known what decisions were made as a result of that trip, but access to the mines from Elkhorn continued to be by trail—not wagon road—for ten more years.

The newspaper story offers an admirable description of the two Elkhorn ranches:

Tel and Jennie May Pope's homestead, post office, and pack station, c. 1905. The nearly treeless mountainsides give testimony to the forest fires that burned parts of the North Fork in the 1800s and early 1900s. (*Photo courtesy of North Santiam Historical Society, Mill City, Oregon and Carl Pope, a descendant.*)

> The Darlings and Popes are grand entertainers. They are among the last families of ranchers on the North Fork, have comfortable homes, large barns, good gardens and fine crops of hay, oats and vegetables, cattle, horses and goats. They provide camping parties with provisions, supply hunting and fishing, act as guides and furnish pack horses.

The Popes had earlier diversified their enterprise by providing pack station services for miners. Now they (and their neighbors, the Darlings) provided outfitter services: hosting and supplying the needs of recreation users such as hunters, fishers, and campers.

Early miners and settlers along the North Fork faced many challenges but forged their lives with independence, resourcefulness, and self-reliance. Those who chose to settle here built their homes and established productive ranches. As roads and bridges improved, they built schools and raised families.

Some like the Taylors, Darlings, Popes, and even the Smiths in Mehama were ahead of their time, catering to the needs of recreationists coming up the North Fork. They likely never imagined how filling the needs of outdoor recreation seekers foretold a time when the canyon would become a prized recreation area. Within a few years, more and more people would come seeking places to fish, swim, explore, and recuperate with a "spell in the woods"—in the health-giving mountains of the North Fork.

9
Fire, Logging, and Conservation

Lightning struck Mother Lode Mountain 1 mile north of the North Fork watershed in 2011, starting a fire in the Bull of the Woods Wilderness. This was during the time I worked for the Oregon Department of Forestry, and I remember ODF fire managers talking through strategies to protect the private lands along the North Fork should the fire threaten there. The fire burned several thousand acres in the Bull of the Woods area and had potential to burn into the North Fork canyon, but the dedicated work of firefighters and the arrival of fall rains prevented further spread.

Even more recently, a dark thunder cell moved up the canyon in 2017, and I watched a bolt of lightning strike Elkhorn Mountain just south of our cabin. With road access close to the blaze, fire fighters quickly built containment lines and helicopters dropped bucketloads of water on the fire. No strong winds came that year to fan the fire, and it never burned out of control. A fire crew continued to watch over the site until the fall rains came.

Since I was a boy, I understood that forest fires had burned along the North Fork in the past, and these recent fires served as sobering reminders that fires could come again—maybe soon—to the forests of the North Fork. I wanted to learn more about the canyon's fire history.

SHAPED BY FIRE

When homesteaders first entered the North Fork watershed, they found themselves surrounded by vast evergreen forests of Douglas-fir, western hemlock, and western redcedar. They passed groves of massive trees, some five hundred to eight hundred years old, as well as smaller younger stands where intense fires had burned the old trees in more recent years. During my lifetime, groves of the ancient trees that had been spared from fire became part of the canyon's mystique.

Opal Creek Ancient Forest Center records show large wildfires along the North Fork in 1550 and again in 1835. Early settlers reported a fire in Elkhorn Valley in 1903.[1] Forest Service records show a fire on Battle Ax mountain in 1908 and two lightning-caused fires in the lower North Fork canyon in 1918. One of the 1918 fires was on the slopes of Lookout Mountain near where our cabin was later built.[2] Growing up in the 1960s, I saw the large silver snags from the 1918 fire still standing on the steep, rocky slopes of the mountain.

Early settlers described a large fire that approached the canyon from the north in 1929. As it came closer to the North Fork, local residents voiced concerns it would burn local mills, including the North Fork's Freres Mill and Crabtree Mill.[3] Another record shows a smaller fire just south of the Little North Fork along Tumble Creek in 1941.[4] These fires typically burned in late summer and continued until fall rains arrived.

One of the best-documented fires was the Sardine Creek Fire of 1951. While forestry records carry only basic references to the fire, newspaper accounts from the time and longtime residents tell a more detailed story.

The fire started in late August, just over the ridge from the North Fork, south of Opal Lake. Believed to have been human-caused, the fire started in a logging area and spread to the surrounding forest. The Albany *Democrat-Herald* reported it grew slowly for more than three weeks but "roared out-of-control" a month later when a 30 mile-per-hour wind blew in from the east. A mechanic at the logging site said he saw "hemlocks two feet in diameter snap off like twigs when struck by the searing flames." Firefighters said the fire raced 8 miles in less than five hours during the night along the ridge between the main North Santiam River and the North Fork. An official feared that "the fiercely burning fire would jump to the north side of the ridge and threaten the settlement of Elkhorn." North Fork residents were warned of the potential danger, and some left their homes.[5]

Several hundred firefighters worked the fire. Blowing embers started spot fires 3 miles ahead, forcing firefighters to abandon their equipment and race down the narrow mountain roads through smoke and ash to escape. Gates residents evacuated during the night as fire approached from three sides.

Along the North Fork, the Bickett family could see the flames on the mountains above them. Firefighters set up a fire camp in their hay field in Elkhorn Valley for trucks, equipment, and workers. Phyllis and Alice Bickett were schoolgirls at the time and told me they remembered the busy fire camp and embers flying through the air that started spot fires in Elkhorn Valley.[6]

Smoke and ash poured into the Willamette Valley. The Albany newspaper reported, "A deep red sun this morning was caused by the heavy pall of yellow smoke that hangs over most of the central Willamette Valley." The Sardine Fire burned through more than 21,000 acres, but the North Fork canyon was spared.

The similarities between this fire and the 2020 Beachie Creek Fire are chilling. The Sardine Creek Fire could have easily burned downslope into the North Fork, but the east winds were not nearly as strong as those in 2020.

As I pieced these fire stories together, the pattern became clear: frequent fires burned in and around the North Fork in decades and centuries past—caused by lightning and Native burning. These recurrent blazes kept flammable undergrowth and dead wood from accumulating on the forest floor. With thick fire-resistant bark and limited burnable material on the ground, the largest trees often survived. Fire shaped the forests into a patchwork pattern such that younger trees became established in burned areas while larger trees—spared from fires—continued to grow, sometimes for centuries and to enormous size. While the canyon's geography had been shaped by volcanoes, glaciers, and landslides, the forests that greeted homesteaders had been shaped in large part by fire.

THE BEGINNINGS OF FOREST CONSERVATION

North America's vast forests became a valued resource for the expanding nation. Through the 1700s and 1800s, lumbermen cut forests across the United States at a rapid pace. Unregulated for years, and viewed as reckless by many, the timber boom of that time eventually gave rise to guidelines for forest conservation and policies for environmental protection.[7]

Gifford Pinchot (1865–1946), a Pennsylvanian, advocated for sustainable management in the nation's forests. Born in Iowa, Aldo Leopold (1887–1948), spoke out for conservation of wildlife. Rachel Carson (1907–1964) of Pennsylvania, famous for her book *Silent Spring*, exposed the damaging effects of chemical pesticides. California's John Muir

(1838–1914) led efforts to protect special areas as national parks. These individuals, along with many others, helped the nation understand the importance of looking after our land and its resources.

Oregon had its own champion for conservation in those days: John Breckenridge Waldo. Born to Oregon pioneers in 1844, Waldo grew up in what is now called the Waldo Hills (named for his family) about 20 miles west of the North Fork. After studying law, he served in the Oregon Supreme Court and State House of Representatives. Suffering from asthma, Waldo retreated to the Cascades for thirty summers to escape the Willamette Valley heat, often on trips of two months or more. The mountain air provided relief, and his extensive mountain exploring made him intimately familiar with the forests and mountains of Santiam country.

On an 1893 mountain trip, Waldo wrote that he saw "the blue water of a lake gleaming from out of the depths of the forest." His group named it Wells Lake after one of the men in the party. Years later, the lake was renamed to what it is called today: Opal Lake, part of the Opal Creek Wilderness.[8]

Representative Waldo introduced a bill to the state legislature in 1891 to establish a state forest reserve along the crest of the Cascade Range. His goal was to protect the things he had come to prize: the beauty of the mountains, wildlife habitat, watersheds for cities and irrigation, high-country huckleberry fields for both Native people and settlers, and "the healthfulness" of the mountain's atmosphere.

The bill gained approval in the House but failed in the Senate, reportedly because of opposition from sheepherders who ran flocks in the mountain meadows. Undeterred, a group of Oregon citizens—including Waldo—successfully advocated for federal designation of a reserve in the Cascade Range that included lands in the upper North Fork canyon. In 1893, President Grover Cleveland established the Cascade Range Forest Reserve to protect watersheds from flooding and erosion and prevent the overexploitation of forests, much as Waldo had originally proposed. Judge Waldo's dream had become a reality, and forests of the upper North Fork received their first official conservation protection.[9]

In 1905, Congress established the US Forest Service, and President Theodore Roosevelt placed the new federal agency in charge of the forest reserves, which were soon renamed national forests. The upper half of the North Fork canyon became part of the Willamette National Forest.

Not only a major advocate of forest conservation, Waldo also supported protection of Crater Lake as a national park. His love for the mountains and forests of Oregon embraced both the ideas of conservation and protection of special places. Waldo is buried in Pioneer Cemetery in Salem, near the graves of Mehama and James Smith. Waldo Lake in the Willamette National Forest is named for him, and a street near my home carries the family name. I'm reminded of John Breckenridge Waldo's love for Oregon's forests and his passion for conservation every time I walk on that street.

Judge John Breckenridge Waldo (1844–1907). Photograph by Andrew and Louis Siegmund. (*Photo courtesy of State Library of Oregon and Lou Siegmund, a descendant.*)

In an ironic twist, while Waldo and others worked to protect Oregon's public forests, others were engaged in an elaborate—but little known—scheme to defraud the US government of publicly owned forests in western Oregon, including thousands of acres in the lower North Fork canyon.

The scheme grew out of an 1870 land grant that transferred vast areas of federal lands to the Oregon-California Railroad Company (the O & C) for construction of a new railroad from Portland to San Francisco. The company was granted 3.7 million acres in western Oregon by the US government and was authorized in turn to sell 160-acre parcels for not more than $2.50 an acre to qualified individuals. This reasonable price was intended to encourage families to settle and develop the area. Proceeds from the sales were to be used to build the railroad while allowing for the O & C to earn a profit for their work. Some land was sold to settlers in the manner agreed to, but other land that contained valuable timber was sold for higher prices to timber companies, with the extra profits going to the pockets of the fraudsters. A 1908 book that describes the scheme, titled *Looters of the Public Domain*, was written by one of the jailed schemers.[10]

The railroad was completed, but because of the fraud, parcels remaining unsold were reconveyed back to public ownership, including nearly 10,000 acres within the lower North Fork canyon. Today these lands are managed by the federal Bureau of Land Management (BLM) and are often referred to as BLM's "O & C Lands." Out of this deceptive plot to benefit a few individuals and timber companies, thousands of acres of forest were eventually placed in the federal agency to be managed for a variety of public benefits including timber production, conservation, water, wildlife, and recreation.

With increasing focus on conservation, Oregon Governor Oswald West signed legislation in 1911 that led to creation of the Oregon Department of Forestry, an agency that exists today. The new department was initially charged with protecting forests from fire, including forests along the North Fork, but its responsibilities later expanded to include broad stewardship of land, water, and wildlife resources. These state-managed lands within the lower part of the North Fork watershed are now part of the Santiam State Forest. Having worked for the Oregon Department of Forestry and listened while managers worked through major decisions, I understand their challenge to balance diverse goals.

Today all forest lands of the North Fork watershed, including Willamette National Forest lands, BLM's O & C lands, and Santiam State Forest lands are managed under a variety of guidelines to provide for conservation of resources including clean water, wildlife habitat, cultural resources, timber, and recreation.

Conservation policies—often controversial—have evolved through the years, and I am certain they will continue to shift over time. Public input will be important, helping managers develop the best policies for managing and looking after the many resources on public lands.

EARLY LOGGING AND LUMBER MILLS

Commercial logging operations began in the North Fork canyon in 1912, when the Silver Falls Timber Company to the north constructed a system of rail lines to haul logs from the remote mountains to its mill. Maps of the time reveal that one or more lines crossed over from the Silver Falls area into the North Fork watershed, where trees were cut and hauled by steam locomotive to the mill near Silverton.[11]

Ten years later, a young entrepreneur named Ted Freres opened a sawmill within the North Fork canyon.[12] At about the same time, Mandy Frank established a mill in Elkhorn Valley, upriver from the Freres operation.[13] The Frank mill was the one my family used to see on the way to our cabin when I was young.

Within a few years, Ted and Mandy formed a partnership and purchased timbered land along the North Fork from the Hammond Lumber Company, a large, multistate mill operation located just to the north, in Mill City. The two men worked together at Elkhorn until the mid-1940s when they dissolved their partnership and divided their assets.[14] Each went on to form their own companies, today known as Freres Lumber Company of Lyons and Frank Lumber Company of Mill City. Both companies became large employers and have continued some of their operations and land holdings along the North Fork.[15]

In addition to the Frank and Freres mills, local residents say a dozen or more small mills operated along the North Fork through the 1930s and 1940s, and most are now all but forgotten. Yet one of them left behind more photographs and information about its history than all the others combined—the Crabtree Mill.

One of the most memorable experiences while doing research on the North Fork was sparked when I made the presentation at the Gates Fire Hall for the North Santiam Historical Society in 2016. I told the audience that I was early in my process and would love to talk with anyone with knowledge about North Fork history. I showed a faded photograph of a lumber mill I had come across at the local museum and confessed that I didn't know anything about it except I understood that it had been located along the North Fork. A hand shot up in the back of the room and a gentle male voice was heard, "I can tell you all about that mill. That was the Crabtree Mill. I was born there and my father was one of the owners."

The voice belonged to Dale Kirsch, retired longtime hardware store owner in Mill City, in his eighties. That evening began a friendship between us; not long afterward I met his brother Gordon, also in his eighties. During get-togethers with Dale in Mill City and Gordon in Salem, I viewed handfuls of photos and heard dozens of stories about the Crabtree Mill. I learned a lot about early logging along the North Fork from these brothers who carried a deep sense of pride in their family history along the North Fork.

Crabtree Lumber Mill on the North Fork, c. 1930s. This is the photo I showed at the historical society's evening program in 2016. (*Photo courtesy of Terry Gookin.*)

Dale and Gordon reported that the lumbering operation was started by three men who got together in 1925 to set up the mill along the North Fork, just upstream from Taylor's Grove. Ira Kirsch (their father), and Ira's brother Paul joined Everett Crabtree to form Crabtree Lumber Company.

Everything ran on steam power. Called a planer mill, the operation cut logs into rough lumber and workers ran it through a planer to give it a smooth finish. The owners built a self-contained village around the mill that included several homes, a cook shack, bunkhouses, and other buildings. The Crabtree employed fourteen mill workers and twenty-one woodsmen who cut old-growth logs with crosscut saws and delivered them to the mill. Constructing a railroad would have been too costly for a small outfit like the Crabtree, so crews hauled the logs using a 1923 hard-tired Garford truck that was started with a crank.[16]

Giant steam-powered winches called steam donkeys pulled ("yarded") logs to the truck. Commonly used in logging operations of the day, the technology replaced horses and oxen used in earlier years. Logs were brought in on a wood plank road that ended on a hill above the mill pond. As the truck rolled into position, a worker released the load and the logs spilled down into the pond.

According to Dale, the average log was 5 feet in diameter, with some up to 8 feet—so large that often the loads came out as "one log loads." One, he remembered, "must have been 12 feet in diameter. The tree was so big and heavy the truck couldn't carry anything longer than an eight-foot section of the log at a time."

Despite the hardships of the Great Depression, the Crabtree was self-contained and able to continue operations even when most other mills shut down. Because there wasn't much cash around, the Crabtree owners bartered lumber for supplies that they used for operations and to give to workers and their families in place of salary. As Dale told me, "Times were tough, but there was work to do, running water in the cabins, and food on the table—and that was saying something in those days."[17]

The mill closed in 1937 when the available timber nearby had been cut. About the time the North Fork mills shut down, some of the privately

The Garford logging truck, with wooden spokes on the front wheels, c. 1928. After a day of challenging physical work in the woods, the Crabtree woodsmen gathered their lunch buckets and jumped on the back of the Garford for a ride back to the mill. (*Photo courtesy of Terry Gookin.*)

owned lands in the lower canyon came into public ownership. These lands had belonged to larger lumber companies like the Hammond Lumber Company and the Silver Falls Timber Company, but when their mills closed, owners deemed some their logged lands to be worth less than the taxes they owed, so they defaulted on their tax payments and ceded the properties to the county. In following years, the county transferred the properties to the Oregon Department of Forestry with the agreement that part of the revenue from future timber harvest would be returned to the county, a policy that continues to this day.

The North Fork mills are gone now and are remembered only through stories and photographs. Yet one piece of the North Fork's early logging story lives on—the old Garford truck from the Crabtree Mill. When the truck was put up for sale in the 1960s, a young automobile restorer—by coincidence a former high school classmate of mine—Terry Gookin, purchased it. Unknown to me, all through the years Terry had watched over the old truck. In recent years, Terry and his friend Al Ketchum have co-owned the truck and worked hard to restore it. Although Terry and I hadn't been in touch for many years, the old truck brought us back together.

In 2018, we invited Dale Kirsch to see "the ol' Garford" that he would have seen as a young boy at the mill. Walking into Terry's shop, Dale's eyes opened wide as he took his first glance at the truck. He slowly ran his hand along its side, recalling out loud how it used to rumble along the plank roads near the mill on the North Fork. I noticed him staring at the original solid-rubber tires, cracked but still functional all these years later. He told us he hadn't seen the truck since it was hauling logs at the Crabtree more than seventy years earlier.

After looking over the truck and snapping photos, we headed to the North Fork, where Dale guided us to the site of the old mill. Nothing was left except a few old pieces of rusting metal. Trees had closed in to become a dense forest, and private homes at the site limited where we could walk. Dale located a spring of cold water, still running strong—and identified it as the spring that had provided water for his family's home. We spotted some daffodils in bloom, marking the site of a home that once stood on the grounds.

The experiences of that day proved powerful for all of us, each in our own way. Dale was thrilled to see the old Garford again, Terry and Al were pleased to see where their truck had been used in the early 1900s, and I was given the gift of learning some of the area's logging history exactly where it happened and from a man who experienced it during an earlier time in North Fork history.[18]

I deeply value the times I shared with Dale and Gordon. While meeting with Dale at his family's restaurant in Mill City some weeks later, he proudly showed me his photos of the mill on the restaurant walls and welcomed me to use the photos in my book. He shared many stories, often with a shine in his eye. He loved history and freely shared what he knew. Like so many others who have told me their North Fork stories, Dale is gone now. He passed away not long after our trip to the old mill site.

Likewise, when meeting with Gordon in his senior apartment in Salem, he always insisted on treating me to lunch in the facility's dining room. As the room emptied out, it would just be Gordon and me sitting together, talking about the old days. One afternoon he invited me to see some photos in his room and proudly showed me seven large framed Crabtree Mill photos on the wall of his small living room. He gazed out the window as he described each photograph, as if still seeing the mill outside as he talked. As Gordon finished describing the photos, he told me a story.

Although he lived at the mill as a boy, where he saw the trucks come and go, the steam rising from the mill, and the men working, he had never really understood how the mill worked. That changed early one morning when his father invited him to come out to the mill. It was time for Gordon to learn about the operation.

To enable little Gordon to see the equipment inside the mill, his dad had him bend his arms at the elbows and stiffen them. His father stood behind and carefully lifted the young boy into the air by the elbows, giving him a good view of everything.

His father explained how everyone worked together to make the mill work. He gestured to where men brought in the logs from the mill pond and drew them through the large circular saw blades to make the rough lumber. He described the planer used to smooth the rough boards into finished lumber. He showed where the finished lumber was loaded onto the trucks to be hauled to town and where the scraps were sent out to be burned. A worker blew a steam whistle with a loud blast. As his dad finished his lesson, the man blew it again, this time with two loud sharp blasts. Gordon watched the machinery burst into motion.

Inside the Crabtree Mill, c. 1930s. (*Photo courtesy of Iva Vanbeek.*)

As his dad lowered him to the ground, Gordon asked permission to blow the whistle. His dad responded with a firm "no," explaining that it could be blown only at certain times and in certain ways. If the whistle was blown in any other way it could result in someone being seriously hurt.

Gordon remembered that conversation vividly, more than seventy years later. He said he had learned about the mill—and a lesson about life: Work together. Do your part. Follow the same rules—and look out for each other.[19] It was the last time I saw Gordon. He passed away a short time later.

Even with the era of small canyon mills drawing to a close, logging in North Fork forests continued, with logs hauled to larger mills in nearby towns. A greater percentage of the forest was now in public ownership, and forest management included guidelines for conservation of resources while still providing a flow of logs to area mills. Within the canyon's fire-shaped forests, logging and conservation had become parallel stories in North Fork history.

10
Tree Army Boys and Cloud Girls

As I ventured on my career working on forest, park, and wilderness lands of the United States, I found myself following paths walked in years past by workers in the Civilian Conservation Corp (the CCC). Now, after more than thirty years surrounded by the CCC legacy in these places of work, I wanted to know what projects, if any, CCC crews might have undertaken along the North Fork.

When the Great Depression hit the United States, mines and mills along the North Fork shut down and jobs were hard to find in the Santiam Canyon. Nationwide, people lived with tremendous hardship. Few were as fortunate as workers at the Crabtree Mill, where the Kirsch brothers managed to keep the mill running and the men working.

In response to the national crisis, President Franklin D. Roosevelt established the Civilian Conservation Corps in 1933. A champion of conservation and environmental protection, Roosevelt had already advocated for numerous conservation bills while serving in state government in New York. The establishment of Roosevelt's Civilian Conservation Corps was aimed at advancing conservation and giving hope to a hurting country.

Part of the national legislation known as the New Deal, the CCC offered outdoor manual labor jobs to unemployed men. Between 1933 and 1942, physically demanding jobs provided a kind of nature-immersion fitness program during which crews lived in rustic camps and worked in conservation-related jobs. Some "CCC boys" built roads, trails, and bridges in the nation's public forests and parks, while others constructed ranger stations and park buildings, fought forest fires, planted trees, and built fire lookouts on remote mountaintops. With so much work connected to the country's forest lands, the boys were sometimes called "Roosevelt's Tree Army" or "Tree Army Boys."

My first job with the US Forest Service in Idaho's Sawtooth National Forest was headquartered at an old ranger station constructed by CCCers. Later, on the Wenatchee National Forest in Washington, I gathered my tree-planting gear each morning at the Leavenworth Ranger Station, built by the Tree Army Boys. When I worked at the Mount St. Helens National Volcanic Monument, I learned about CCC projects there. At the Tillamook Forest Center, we told visitors about the Tree Army that planted trees after the Tillamook Burn. Even at Hawai'i Volcanoes National Park, I lived in a CCC-built cottage for a time and worked in the Kīlauea Visitor Center, a wood and stone structure constructed by the men.

Through the years, I recalled locals saying the CCCers had built the original bridge over Gold Creek in the upper North Fork canyon. But was this true? If so, had they also done other work in the canyon? I met with Cara Kelly, cultural resource assistant at the Detroit Ranger Station, just over the ridge from the North Fork, who pulled up files for me confirming what I had heard: the CCCs had indeed worked along the North Fork.[1]

I contacted the Forest History Center, situated on the campus of the Oregon Department of Forestry in Salem where Oregon's CCC history takes center stage. ODF historian Alan Maul led me up the narrow stairway of the CCC-built structure that houses the center's exhibits. We sat down at his computer and Alan looked over his shoulder at me.

"You know, the administrative work supporting the CCCs up the Santiam was handled right here in this building. ODF has restored it inside and out, so this is what the office would have looked like in the '30s when Santiam workers came to town."[2]

I learned that two large camps in Mill City and Gates housed men for projects in the Willamette National Forest. Then Alan surprised me when he added, "I see there was also a smaller remote camp upstream from Elkhorn. It would have provided a base for CCC projects in the national forest lands of the North Fork canyon." He pulled up a Forest Service newsletter from 1933 describing the North Fork camp. The camp was called Camp Mehama, and the newsletter read, "The camp is both beautiful and convenient. A cold, rushing mountain stream, the Little North Fork Santiam, sings its way by on one side, and [mountains rise] on the other."[3]

This was a breakthrough. Not only had the CCCers worked during the day along the North Fork, they lived at a small camp in the canyon!

A report about the Mill City Camp revealed that four hundred enrollees and officers had arrived from Chicago in 1934, and about half of them were sent to work along the upper North Fork. Half of the enrollees were so-called colored men, revealing the policy to forbid discriminatory practices based on "race, color, or creed."[4] Arriving in the wildlands of the North Fork must have awakened a new sense of wonder for many of the men, who may have known very little about the mountains and forests of the Pacific Northwest.

CCC boys at the North Fork Camp worked on a range of projects similar to those of other Cascade-based crews. US Forest Service records confirmed they did build the first bridge over Gold Creek in 1934, as I had heard from locals. Constructed with old-growth Douglas-fir logs nearly 80 feet long and more than 3 feet in diameter, the bridge must have been a major engineering feat, as it required placing the logs across the canyon with cascading water far below. The enrollees also built a narrow road from the Jawbone Flats Mining Camp to Battle Ax mountain. Later washed out in many places and maintained as a hiking trail, the old road is still sometimes referred to as the "Government Road" because of its origin.

The Tree Army boys built the Pearl Creek Guard Station at the base of Henline Mountain, a remote North Fork outpost from which the Forest Service conducted fire patrols, maintained trails, and built fire lookouts. This guard station had been a favorite canyon feature of mine since childhood, but I never knew it had been built by the CCCers.

Digging deeper into Forest Service records, I learned about the towering presence of Roy Elliott, district ranger at the nearby Detroit Ranger Station for thirteen years, until 1935. With a large stature and powerful job, Elliott exercised dominion over large swaths of forest (including the upper North Fork canyon), and he presided over much of the local CCC enrollee's work. Working throughout the district as woodsman and boss enabled him to get to know the canyon well. He came to especially love a small tributary called Boulder Creek and is said to have commented, "The only thing more beautiful than Boulder Creek is my wife." Forest Service records show he later changed the creek's name to Opal Creek in honor of his wife Opal. The name stuck.[5]

Starting with the early years of the US Forest Service, leaders determined that aggressive fire suppression was the right approach for protecting the new national forests. They set out to establish fire lookout stations

Ranger Roy Elliott (*left*) and a Civilian Conservation Corps crew in the Willamette National Forest, c. 1933. (*US Forest Service photo.*)

on the tops of high peaks from which fires could be spotted quickly. Enrollees became a crucial work force for building the structures, and for fighting the fires once they were spotted. The boys built a trail up Henline Mountain in 1934 and constructed a lookout at the top. Besides the Henline Lookout, CCC boys built four other lookouts on mountains surrounding the North Fork (a sixth lookout on Battle Ax mountain had been constructed prior to the CCC era).[6]

At an elevation of just over 4,000 feet, the Henline Mountain Lookout held a commanding view of nearly all of the North Fork watershed. Constructed on a stone foundation, it was painted light green inside and silver-gray outside, standard lookout colors at that time. A wire phone line was strung up the trail from tree to tree, from Pearl Creek Guard Station to the lookout and from the Henline Lookout to other nearby lookouts. When I walked the Henline Mountain Trail in recent years, I sometimes spotted evidence of the old phone line that once carried important fire reports through the forest.

As far back as I can remember, I was fascinated with the Henline Mountain Lookout. From our cabin I could see its roofline on a large exposed rock atop the mountain. One day when I was young, the man who worked in the lookout walked down the mountain and along the road to Elkhorn. He stopped across the river from our cabin and waved. My dad climbed aboard our raft and brought him across to the cabin for a visit. He told all about his work in the lookout. As a young boy, I was captivated by this man who lived alone atop the mountain.

By 1942, with World War II raging, Congress redirected funding for the program toward the war effort. CCC camps closed, and many of the enrollees joined the military. The work in the Civilian Conservation Corps had provided excellent physical and mental training for the soon-to-be soldiers. But the nation's legacy of conservation didn't end with the CCC camp closures—women answered the call for help.

"CLOUD GIRLS" WATCH OVER THE FORESTS

Through Forest Service records, I learned about Dorothy Gray Middleton, a young woman who volunteered as a fire watcher at the Battle Ax Mountain Lookout Station in 1943. Perched at almost 6,000 feet elevation, her lookout featured an upper floor cupola with maps and fire-finding equipment that served as the observation post. Her rustic living quarters were on the lower level.

Dorothy's remote post was one of the many lookout jobs filled by women when men left to serve in World War II. Because of their work on the high and sometimes cloud-covered mountain tops, the women came to be known as the Cloud Girls. Although she was a member of the Salem-based Chemeketans hiking club and not new to roughing it, she found the job on this remote mountain top demanding from sunup to sundown. She quipped about the experience in her journal:

> It is a summer hotel so exclusive that not money but qualification limits the clientele. The bus service is terrible. You have to walk and climb and carry your belongings, your food and all the extras on your own back. You gather your own fuel, stoke your own fires,

Battle Ax Fire Lookout, 1943. Perched more than a mile high on the old volcano, the lookout offered a 360-degree view of the Cascades, with the North Fork watershed directly west. Dorothy Middleton, who may be a worker in this photograph, described her view of five snow-capped volcanic peaks, from Mount Rainer to Mount Jefferson, as a "convention of giants." (*Photo courtesy of the Oregon Department of Forestry, Forest History Center, Salem, Oregon, and the US Forest Service.*)

> cook your own meals. You haul water in small quantities up a steep grade. You love every bit of it.

Dorothy continues,

> None of the bedrooms has beautyrests. There is one bed, the springs are of rope. You are your own maid. During lightning storms and bad fire weather, you might not even have time to do much cooking or get too much sleep. You are too busy watching, sighting, and reporting to your Operations.

Dorothy artfully described her environment:

> If I have wondered why they pay anybody for spending a vacation watching over this beautiful country, I know now. With me, the

> pay is all for washing windows. I am cleaning the canvas on our panoramic views. These murals are lovely and all the care they require of me is this Monday cleaning, and constant guard against complete destruction by flame.[7]

Dorothy Middleton and other Cloud Girls played an important role keeping watch over the nation's forests when life was already challenging because of the Depression and the war. Dorothy's writings portray her joy in the work and demonstrated that women were readily called to work in lookouts that were up to this time typically staffed by men.[8]

While the Tree Army Boys and the Cloud Girls worked only a few short years, their legacy lives on in public lands across the country. Like the ranger stations and park buildings I worked in during my career, many of the CCC-built ranger stations, work centers, and visitor centers across the nation are still used and celebrated. The lodge at Silver Falls State Park northeast of Salem is a strikingly beautiful example located nearby.[9] Some fire lookouts are still used for their original purpose, while others (like the Gold Butte Lookout just east of Battle Ax mountain) have been decommissioned and converted to nostalgic and rustic mountaintop recreation rentals.

Through my lifetime on the North Fork, CCC history was all around me. As I peered through windows of the Pearl Creek Guard Station during my early years, crossed the Gold Creek bridge, walked the trails, and stood beside the Henline Mountain Lookout, I was experiencing the work of the Tree Army and the Cloud Girls—but I had not heard their North Fork stories until many years later. Their work across the United States during challenging times reflected the nation's growing interest in conservation, and their projects along the North Fork contributed to the tradition of people looking after the lands, forests, and waters of the canyon.

11
A Modern-Day Parable

I had nearly missed one of the most important sources of stories from Santiam country because I had not been able to locate the legendary woman I had heard so much about. Several locals had told me I had to talk to a woman named Iva VanBeek because she had lived in the area all her life and knew a lot about local history. I had tried numerous times to locate her, but nobody knew where she lived or how to contact her. Just as I was about to give up trying to find her, someone advised, "talk to Pastor Troy at the Mehama Community Church, he'll know how to reach her." Knowing Troy from our bell-tower-climbing adventure the year before, I gave him a call. Within a few days we were sitting down with Iva. She had been there under my nose the whole time, living in a house just outside the town of Mehama. I could see on first meeting that more than nine decades of life had not affected Iva's memory; it seemed as solid as the young girl that she was in the 1920s, and her stories seemed ready to flow as soon as someone would ask her to tell them. Indeed, Iva opened up a deep oral history and uncovered a rich collection of photos, including ones taken and developed by her father John.[1]

Iva VanBeek had a quick wit and easy laugh. Sitting with the ninety-four-year-old in her living room, I found myself lost in her sense of humor and colorful language as she described early life in Mehama in vivid detail. Family photos and a painting of the house she had grown up in hung on the walls. A nearby table made by her grandfather held stacks of holiday greeting cards and letters from friends.

Of all the stories Iva shared during our delightful meetings at her home, the accounts that brought out her sense of delight the most were about her parents, John and Jennie Moe. The stories helped me to visualize what it was like for a family facing opportunities and challenges of life in rural Oregon in the early 1900s. As compelling as almost anything else

John and Jennie Moe and a daughter (on right) at their homestead, c. 1910. Person on left has not been identified. (*Photo courtesy of Iva Vanbeek.*)

I learned during my research, these stories stitched together many aspects of North Fork history I had been learning.

So, who were John and Jennie Moe?

John and Jennie came to Oregon as newlyweds from a tiny hamlet in Wisconsin in 1908. He was twenty-five, she was twenty. They stayed briefly in Silverton, about 20 miles from Mehama, where John's parents had arrived two years earlier. For a while John and Jennie lived in a shack, although they didn't own it and, according to Iva, didn't know who did. In 1909 they moved to the southern branch of the Santiam River where they established a homestead. They built a house, barn, and chicken house, and established an apple orchard and a huge garden. They eventually had four daughters. Jennie carried much of the weight at the homestead while John worked as what Iva called a "charter member of the newly minted US Forest Service" on the Santiam National Forest, later named the Willamette National Forest.

John Moe, c. 1920. He called this photo "On the Lookout." (*Photo courtesy of Iva Vanbeek.*)

John built trails, strung telephone line, planted trees, and did whatever else was needed by the new federal agency. His work lay in the forests of both the North and South Santiam Rivers. At times John worked with Roy Elliott, who was later appointed district ranger.

From 1911 to 1920, John spent summers on the summit of Tidbits Mountain (some 40 miles south of Mehama), where he manned the fire lookout station, one of the first in Oregon. During breaks, he trekked 20 miles through the forest to be picked up at the nearest road.

By 1922, the Moe's three oldest daughters were school-age, but with no schoolhouse near the homestead, Jennie felt they needed to move. John loved his job and hated the thought of leaving their home but realized that Jennie was right. They moved back to Silverton, where their fourth daughter Iva was born.

John took temporary work in Silverton as a mechanic; he was good at repairing engines on trucks and cars that were now becoming mainstream in the United States. He heard talk of a new highway that would take travelers from Salem over the Cascades to Central Oregon through the town of Mehama. He envisioned opening an auto and truck repair shop along the new highway. The Moes moved to Mehama.

As the family settled, an unexpected opportunity came along for John: work as the mechanic for the Crabtree Mill, just up the road from town. With this job he could work in the forests of the North Fork during the day and drive home to his family in the evening. It was an ideal arrangement for a man who loved both his family and working in the woods.

John's role as mill mechanic was critical to the operation. He kept the machinery and trucks running and would have known the old Garford well. Iva remembered making trips out to the mill with her dad, including one time when her mom fell from a nearby bridge into the North Fork. Iva said, "Dad jumped in with her to be sure she got out okay."

At their new home, Jennie established a large garden and canned much of her produce in a big copper kettle. She made clothes for their girls using her treadle sewing machine. The girls walked to school during the week, and the whole family walked to the Presbyterian Church for Sunday services. The four young girls had lots of friends who called them the "Moe-Lasses." Iva said, "That's the way we were, and we loved it. We loved living in Mehama."

Iva told me one of her favorite pastimes as a child was pounding old nails into pieces of wood with a hammer. She recalled one day walking to the local store with her dad. While he was talking with the storekeeper, she saw a bin full of shiny new nails sold by the pound. She picked one up to look at and without thinking slipped it in her pocket. When they got home, the nail was discovered. When he learned she had taken it from the store, he instructed her to return the nail and apologize to the storekeeper. Iva described her dad as a very honest and kind man. "He was teaching me to be honest too." Iva's parents knew how much she loved pounding nails; some weeks later, they gave her a sack of shiny new nails for her birthday. She loved the gift.

Iva remembered when electricity first came to Mehama in 1929. Her family hooked up lights, but the house had no outlets. With a laugh, Iva explained, "We didn't need plug-ins; we didn't have nothin' to plug in!" From that day, life was easier because the family no longer needed to trim the wicks and clean the chimneys on the oil lamps. Even after the power line came to their house, electricity went out a lot during storms. Iva quipped, "Still does."

She also remembered when telephone service came to Mehama and her parents had a phone installed in their home. Iva said that for years she was "scared to death of it" and would not answer it because "it just didn't feel right talking to someone who wasn't there in the room with you." Eventually she did answer the phone sometimes, although she said she never liked to do it. During one of our conversations, Iva's phone rang. She walked over, looked at the caller ID, and didn't answer it. Looking back our way, she said flatly, "Robo call." After a pause and another laugh, she added, "See, I still don't like to answer the phone!" We all laughed.

Iva described the social events her family attended at Oakdale School years ago. People came from all around, and there were lots of pies and talking among neighbors. She remembered that Marion Taylor invariably came with his accordion. Already in his eighties, he was able to play most any songs by request. "That's what people did, and the social gatherings connected people."

Iva remembered that a lot of people still had horses and wagons in the 1930s and that only a few people in town owned cars. She described a rail line from the Silver Falls Timber Company that passed through town and a water tower where the trains stopped to get water for the boilers on the steam engines. She told me about the local CCC camps. She recalled going up the North Fork to the mines "on a very rough road." She told about the old Smith Hotel, although she recalled in later years it became more of a boardinghouse than a hotel. She also remembered when it burned.

Following his years at the Crabtree Mill, John worked as a mechanic for the Freres Lumber Mill and the Silver Falls Timber Company. Iva said her dad liked people and everybody liked him. He had many friends. Her dad caught a terrible cold in the winter of 1936–37. He had been spending long hours on his back on the ground in cold weather while working on trucks. Tragically, he died after several weeks, probably from pneumonia. John Moe was fifty-three.

John's death left Jennie to raise their four daughters in the challenging times of the Great Depression. "We didn't have nothin," Iva recalled, "but nobody else did either." Jennie worked multiple jobs, but money was always tight. She tried to sell some of John's tools to get cash, but no one had enough money to buy them, so she gave the tools away to people who needed them. She took in a foster child while also helping neighbors who were struggling.

Iva remembered when a woman working at the Smith Hotel hurt her back and could not care for her infant. Jennie took care of the child for weeks, accepting no compensation.

One Sunday Jennie realized she only had one dollar to her name but had always put money in the collection plate at church. Without hesitation, she took the dollar and headed for church with the girls. When the offering was taken, she put her dollar in the plate. When the service ended and everyone was leaving for home, Luther Stout, a son of Lewis Stout, told her he wanted to pay her for the tools she had given him months earlier. He reached out his hand and gave her two dollars in payment. Iva said that's how things went for her mom. She worked hard and things always seemed to work out.

Some years after her death, the town of Mehama needed to name a section of the old North Fork Road leading east out of town. The town chose "Jennie Road" to honor the life of Jennie Moe. Experiencing Iva's stories, photographs, and laughter was an extraordinary treat I will never forget. I had first been drawn to her father's experiences with the Forest Service, as he was among the first people to do conservation work in Santiam country and work for one of the first lumbering operations along the North Fork. However, after I learned of John's early death—almost forty years before Jennie's—I was quickly pulled into Jennie's compelling story of raising four daughters on her own during very difficult times.

The things she told me also illustrate how the stories of Mehama and the North Fork tie together with the stories of nearby communities, linking people and small communities to a larger whole. Seeing all of this through Iva's eyes helped me understand the area's history more clearly and appreciate it all more deeply. A few years after meeting Iva, I received news that she had passed away at age ninety-eight.

History can sometimes appear to be mostly about facts and singular events, but the John and Jennie Moe story goes deeper. It shines light on what it was like for a family to live in this area during tough times early in the twentieth century—establishing a home and starting a family, finding work, balancing career with family, adjusting to changes in society, and facing the tragedy of an untimely death. Their story is a modern-day parable, modeling some of the most desirable qualities in our lives together: living honestly and thoughtfully in a community, sharing time with friends and neighbors and helping each other when times are tough. Jennie's story of strength, determination and resilience carried her through the challenges of the time and teaches a timeless lesson for days when we face difficult times again.

12
Primitive Beauty

By the late 1940s and early 1950s, life along the North Fork had begun to change. The era of homesteading and self-reliant ranching, with families living, working, and attending school in the North Fork canyon was drawing to a close.

A headline in the *Oregon Statesman* newspaper on May 3, 1949, read, "Elkhorn, Not a City but a Valley, Holds Its Primitive Atmosphere." Written by Jean Roberts, the article described the wild character of Elkhorn Valley at a time when Willamette Valley residents were just beginning to discover it. It said, "More and more city people are being drawn here by the primitive beauty." My own family would soon join those being drawn to the beauty and wild character of the North Fork.

Jean and her husband Ray Roberts had moved to Elkhorn Valley in 1940 and built a small house on land made available to them by the logging company Ray worked for. A journalist, Jean wrote prolifically for the *Salem Statesman*, the Mill City *Enterprise*, and other local newspapers during the 1940s and 1950s and compiled some of her articles into a book titled *Elkhorn and Mehama*. No longer in print, her book provides an insider's look at the self-sufficient "git-er-done" lives of "North Forkers." We had a copy of the book at the cabin for many years, and our family paged through it so many times the binding fell apart. Much of the North Fork lore I learned as a youngster came from it. Meeting the Roberts' daughter Jo Philippi and her husband Steve became a delightful and meaningful part of my research as they invited me into their North Fork home for coffee. Not only did they share their own canyon stories with me, they opened Jean's archives of writing and photographs and welcomed me to include materials in this book.

Jean's 1949 news story captured changes along the North Fork to a T. Even as the self-reliant ranching era began to close, the canyon's primitive beauty remained, attracting a new era of interest in recreation, parks, summer cabins, and retirement homes.[1]

Not far from the Roberts' cabin, Bill and Millie Bickett still worked their 300-acre ranch in Elkhorn Valley at the bottom of Gates Hill. Together with their daughters Jackie, Phyllis, and Alice, they were the last full-time ranching family along the North Fork. Their ranch featured a classic farmhouse, spacious barn, fruit trees, garden, and large open hay fields on the flat lands that formed when the ancient lake filled with rock and sand millennia ago. Bill worked tirelessly to clear brush and pull out stubborn old-growth tree stumps to maintain and expand their pastures.

I visited with Phyllis and Alice several times in recent years as they spoke fondly of their years on the North Fork. Phyllis attended the old Elkhorn School and said some students walked as far as 5 miles to get there, and at least one boy rode a horse to school. They recalled a community hall by the river where locals gathered for potlucks, dances, and card games. Their parents worked hard to make a living on the ranch but remember their father saying passionately, "I wouldn't trade those years for anything."

Echoing the news article, Phyllis and Alice described how life along the North Fork began to change by the late 1940s. Living in a remote canyon without commercial electricity or phones meant that residents had to know how to accomplish challenging jobs with few outside resources. Most men worked in the woods, drove log trucks, or worked in North Fork sawmills. Only a few still lived and worked at the mines. Although logging was still active, mills along the North Fork had closed. Without the mills, there were fewer and fewer jobs in the canyon, and by 1950, the Elkhorn School closed. Yet, as Jean Roberts' article described, people were now coming out from the Willamette Valley in search of homesites. By mid-century, homes already populated the lower end of the canyon as far as the Oakdale School. Farther up the canyon, one of the first developments came at the site of the old Crabtree Mill. It was purchased and subdivided for housing.[2]

A short distance away, the Taylor family had continued to manage their Taylor's Grove property for picnicking and camping. In view of its popularity, along with increasing public interest in camping and recreation, Marion County sought to purchase it for development as a county park—but no agreement could be worked out. Instead, the land was subdivided and sold for building lots.

Driving up the canyon in the 1950s, my parents sometimes mentioned we were passing Thetford Lodge beside the river. While they seemed to know all about it, I never understood that the lodge hidden in the trees was a family retreat belonging to former Oregon Governor Charles Sprague (1939–1943).

Much of what I learned about the governor's retreat came from Floyd McKay, longtime Oregon journalist and himself an early Elkhorn cabin owner. Sitting with Floyd and his wife Dixie on their deck in 2018, I listened as Floyd described how he had worked for Mr. Sprague at the *Oregon Statesman* newspaper in Salem beginning in 1960. Several times, Floyd referred to the book he had written about the former governor (*An Editor for Oregon: Charles A. Sprague and the Politics of Change*) as he described the man's love for the river.[3]

In the early 1940s, Charles and Blanche Sprague began coming to the canyon for getaways from their fast-paced city lives to visit a friend's cabin near the Crabtree Mill. Sprague loved hiking, mountain climbing, and swimming the chilly water of the North Fork.

The Spragues eventually acquired land upstream from the mill and built their own place they labeled Thetford Lodge, a name associated with Mrs. Sprague's family. Days along the North Fork away from the work world were times the governor could host grandchildren, relax, dress casually, and, as Floyd described, "even go a day without shaving."[4] Nearby residents report that he became such a regular in the canyon that his favorite swimming hole—an enchanting deep pool—became known locally as Governor's Hole.[5]

But the story of Governor Sprague goes beyond his love for the North Fork and having a retreat there: during his years as governor, Sprague advocated for wise management of Oregon's forests. Under his leadership, Oregon became the first state to regulate timber harvest practices on state and private lands. He worked to create a forest research program and rigorous statewide reforestation program. He also worked to establish the Keep Oregon Green Association to advocate for the prevention of human-caused forest fires.[6]

While working for the Oregon Department of Forestry I had learned of Governor Sprague's work to assure that forests were replanted

Governor Charles Sprague, c. 1940. (*Photo courtesy of Oregon Historical Society, Portland, Oregon.*)

following the Tillamook Burn. Not yet aware of his connection to the North Fork, I attended the dedication of a new interpretive sign at the Charles Sprague Memorial Wayside west of Portland in 2012, honoring his conservation legacy.

Later in life, Mr. Sprague joined the Salem-based Chemeketans hiking group and became an advocate for protecting wild places in Oregon, including establishment of the Mount Jefferson Wilderness. As a senior Republican statesman, his backing of wilderness legislation stood as an important endorsement for the wilderness plan.[7] A lake in the Mount Jefferson Wilderness and a Salem high school were named in his honor.

Governor Sprague viewed his conservation actions as investments in Oregon's future and identified forest conservation as one of his personal legacies. Because of his passions, the management of an increasing amount of state and private forest land along the North Fork and throughout Oregon became guided by conservation principles.

Even when advanced age made it difficult for them to hike and climb in the high mountains, the Spragues still retreated to the woods of the North Fork. After enjoying Thetford Lodge for thirty years, they donated it to Willamette University as a retreat center for faculty and students.[8]

By 1944 Kenneth and Frances Randall had moved to Elkhorn, a few miles upriver from Thetford Lodge and the Bickett Ranch. Kenneth's family had been connected to the property since 1915; it was the parcel that Tel and Jennie May Pope had homesteaded and the site of the old Elkhorn Post Office. The first-floor walls of the iconic ranch house were built from logs, and it had a classic covered porch and a metal roof that shed snow in winter. A spring provided fresh water, and a 6-foot fence protected the orchard and garden from deer. The family had recreated at the ranch house in summer and on weekends since the 1930s, but the kids had grown and the Randalls had new plans for the place.[9]

I interviewed their youngest son Craig Z. Randall when he was already nearly ninety. He grew up coming to Elkhorn in the 1930s. Sitting with me in the living room of his historic house, I felt I was in a North Fork Museum. Their old crank telephone hung on the wall where it had been for seventy years, and a colorful braided rug, made by Frances Randall and our friend Mrs. Wheeler filled the living room floor. Between Mr. Randall and I stood a small magazine rack, fashioned from a handmade wooden tool holder once used by ranchers while shoeing horses and mules.

Mr. Randall told me his parents had spent a year renovating the building and opened it in 1945 as a guesthouse, much like a present-day bed and breakfast. The refurbished ranch house had six guest rooms and offered full meals in the dining room that featured Frances's renowned homemade pies. For a time, they hired local teenager Jackie Bickett to work in the kitchen and dining room. People came for the good food and country hospitality, and the chance to hike, fish, and explore.

Elkhorn Guest Ranch, c. late 1940s. (*Photo courtesy of Salem Public Library and the Randall family.*)

A marketing brochure for the Guest Ranch read,

> Spend your vacation at the Elkhorn Guest Ranch, up in the Cascade mountains on the Little North Fork of the Santiam River. The Elkhorn Guest Ranch on the scenic Little North Fork, adjoining the Willamette National Forest, is not a Public Resort but a private place, with a home atmosphere and featuring delicious home cooked meals. You rough it in a plush sort of way. Whether you come for a week-end, a week or a month, there are plenty of streams and lakes to fish, mountain trails to hike and exploring to do that will fill every minute of your time. [10]

Mr. Randall also described that some guests became interested in looking for recreational and retirement property to buy. In time, his parents divided and sold some of their land for building sites.

I didn't realize how fortunate I was to visit Mr. Randall that day in 2015. It was his last visit to Elkhorn and his beloved ranch house. He passed away just a month later.

In the same year the Randalls opened the guest ranch, 1945, five professors and students from Reed College in Portland formed a joint venture company they called the Elkhorn Corporation and purchased 250 acres adjoining the ranch. Within a short time, corporation members began building homes on the property, the first retirement homes at Elkhorn.

Among the original members was Agnes Wheeler, a widow who moved to Elkhorn and in time became a close friend of our family. Old-timers said she helped build her charming home and hand dug the basement herself using a pick, shovel, and wheelbarrow. A former botany major at Reed, Mrs. Wheeler assembled an expansive garden of flowers, shrubs, and trees that resembled a botanical garden. Her blueberry plants produced bumper crops, and her pin oaks blazed orange and red in the fall.

I sometimes helped her with small maintenance projects in her home when I was in high school. I often found myself studying her stunning black-and-white photographs of canyon waterfalls on the walls in her living room. A skilled photographer, she had spent years finding her way to each waterfall, developing and printing the photos herself. She once joked, "I had to hang by eyebrows to get this one."

Mrs. Wheeler, my grandmother, my mother, and me (*left to right.*), c. 1962, in front of Mrs. Wheeler's home. I had already fed the fish and explored the creekside trail, while my mother held the gift of flowers from the garden. (*Photo from author's collection.*)

Although it was on private property, by the mid-1950s, Salmon Falls had become a popular camping and fishing site for Willamette Valley residents. Consistent with the county's interest in park development along the North Fork, park planners negotiated an agreement with the Elkhorn Corporation to purchase the property surrounding the falls and developed it as Salmon Falls County Park.[11]

A short distance from Mrs. Wheeler's, George and Claire Pettingell bought a Randall lot and built a retirement home on a small creek. George was the younger brother of Jennie May Pope, who had homesteaded at Elkhorn. A retired engineer, Pettingell designed a 14-foot water wheel to generate electricity from the creek.[12]

Water flowed down a 200-foot wooden flume from an intake up along the creek to their place. Mr. Pettingell also set up a local system of hand-crank telephones for communication between homes and cabins at Elkhorn. Their unique home was so ingeniously built and beautifully maintained that a Portland home and garden magazine published a story about it. The Pettingells were aways kind to me as a boy and welcomed me to fish in the stream on their property.

While at the Canyon Life Museum in Mill City one morning in 2018, I was looking through old newspapers with Bev Redding, a local history expert and museum volunteer. She had offered to help watch for information related to the North Fork, including about the bright red home called the Cranberry House, whose name had always puzzled me. After an hour combing through the papers, Bev (who has a bubbling fervor about local history) suddenly exclaimed, "Jim, here's a news article about the Cranberry House!"[13]

We found out that Steve and Bonita Meyers purchased the old Elkhorn School in 1954 and moved it across the road, where it became part of their retirement home. Bonita loved a type of red glassware called cranberry glass and had many samples of it in their home. Over the years, this impressive display led to the house's nickname, Cranberry House. Although the house was always painted bright red, I finally understood the real reason the house was called the Cranberry House—and now I also knew what happened to the old Elkhorn School. This unusual house became a well-known Elkhorn landmark in the 1950s and 1960s.

In 1947, Clyde and Laura Everett from Salem bought one of the forested lots from the Randalls and began building a cabin overlooking a wide pool in the river. Many other cabins had been built in the area but had been constructed by homesteaders, miners, and loggers in earlier years. The Everett place was to be a summer cabin—the first real recreation cabin built in Elkhorn Valley.

Over the next couple of years, the Everetts finished construction of their cabin. However, before they'd had much chance to enjoy it, Mr. Everett got a call from his company's home office: they needed him for work in California—right away. The Everetts needed to move, and they would have to let the cabin go. My Dad knew Mr. Everett through the print shop and drove up with him to see the place. Mom was in Minnesota visiting family, but Dad fell in love with the cabin and soon made an offer. Mom always said she took one look at it and fell in love too. My parents never looked back.

The Everetts told Mom and Dad they had "built the cabin around the rhododendron" that grew wild there. They loved native plants and encouraged them not to plant a lawn or do other landscaping that would need to be maintained. Our family always followed their advice. We became regulars, traveling up nearly every weekend during the summers of my youth.

Through all our years going up the North Fork, my family made it a practice to stop and visit neighbors. We became friends with all of them—the Randalls, Mrs. Wheeler, the Pettingells, the McKays, and many others. We typically saw one neighbor on one trip and another neighbor on the next. Even as a young boy I formed special relationships with residents and cabin owners and got to know many of them by name (to me they were mister and missus, of course), and in those early years they knew me as Jimmy.

Looking back, these Elkhorn neighbors were role models in the way they lived with a high level of independence in this remote canyon, as they built and cared for their mountain homes, loved the valley where they lived, celebrated holidays together, and supported each other. When work was needed, everyone pitched in labor or cash (or both) to get the job done. The way our neighbors lived enhanced the beauty of the North Fork and Elkhorn Valley and helped infect me with my love for the North Fork, its people, and the outdoors.

I now see that my family entered the North Fork story when the era of self-sufficient ranches had only recently drawn to a close. Like so many others that followed, we became part of the new recreation era, with interests in fishing, hiking, and exploring the forests and mountains. The "primitive" beauty of the North Fork had become a valued resource not only for us, but for many other Oregonians as well.

13
Things That Came . . . and Things That Almost Did

As my family traveled the rough canyon roads through the 1950s and 1960s, more changes were coming to the North Fork. Some improved the lives of residents and visitors, while others threatened the very qualities that drew them there.

THINGS THAT CAME

While phone service came to the lower canyon as early as the 1920s, local residents say it took until 1955 for a phone line to be strung the rest of the way up to Elkhorn. Unlike the early phones in the lower canyon, the new system meant no more warning tones or cutoffs for exceeding a time limit, but there were still party lines shared between two or more households. Valley Telephone Company ran advertisements reminding callers to cooperate and use party lines "sharingly." One ad read, "Whenever people cooperate, things work smoother, faster, better." The message was universal and timeless.

Through the early 1950s there was still no commercial power in Elkhorn Valley, but that was about to change. President Roosevelt had already made an impact with his Civilian Conservation Corps, but another lesser-known New Deal agency also had significant influence in the canyon: the Rural Electrification Administration, or REA, established in 1936.

While 90 percent of urban households had electricity in the 1930s, only 10 percent of rural homes had the service. The REA sought to reduce rural poverty and improve economic equity—similar to later efforts to

Facing page: Salmon Falls, c. early 1950s. The view of the falls remains unchanged today thanks to the careful work of planners who designed the fish ladder to protect the aesthetic quality of the falls. (*Photo courtesy of North Santiam Historical Society.*)

bring high-speed internet to rural places. The REA provided low-interest loans to rural electric cooperatives to set up and manage electrical service. The REA became one of the most impactful agencies of the New Deal.

Electricity finally reached Elkhorn in 1957 through creation of one of the small electrical cooperatives. Once electricity arrived to our cabin, Dad no longer had to start up the "power plant" and the lights didn't flicker any more. I came to understand the entry that Dad wrote in the cabin journal in bold letters: *"HOOKED UP TO REA!"*

Beginning in the 1960s, road and bridge improvements also began to change life in the North Fork. Marion County replaced the Lomker's timbered bridge with a cement structure, widened narrow road sections, and improved drainage in slide areas.[1] Year by year, the county paved the rough gravel road with asphalt farther and farther up the canyon. Workers rerouted a narrow section of road just downstream from Elkhorn Valley, and as a result, it no longer passed King Tut's Tomb. When the road was straightened at one place, BLM repurposed the abandoned section to become the access road for the new Elkhorn Valley Recreation Site and Campground. Walking along that road in the campground brings back memories of the days when Dad used to drive us through this narrow canyon in the red Buick.[2]

In 1964, a Salem golf devotee fulfilled a dream by purchasing the flat open ranchlands once owned by the Bicketts to build a nine-hole golf course. I remember watching his workers use heavy equipment to uproot 20-foot-tall Douglas-fir trees from surrounding forests and replant them in Bickett's former pastures.[3] There was irony in witnessing the men reverse Mr. Bickett's back-breaking work to remove the trees and stumps only years before. There's further irony too: elk have made this valley their home for centuries, but once the golf course was developed, the iconic animals had to be kept away to keep the greens in top playing condition for golfers.

The electrical service and telephone lines and the straightening and widening of North Fork Road likely eased the burdens of people in the canyon. But humans were not the only ones benefiting from development. The North Fork's wild salmon and steelhead runs also benefited from human intervention. Kalapuyan oral history tells that salmon have long come to the Willamette River and up into the Santiam, seeking the cold waters of the upper canyons.[4] Biologists also believe that fish have come to the Willamette River system for about 15 million years in great numbers. Local old-timers such as Craig Z. Randall have told me about migrating salmon so thick "you could walk across the river on their backs."

However, with fish populations in the Willamette watershed declining in the 1940s, officials looked for ways to restore their numbers. As early as 1949, state fish and game officials began discussing potential for a fish ladder at Salmon Falls since both wild spring Chinook salmon and wild winter steelhead were blocked from passage farther upstream by the 30-foot falls.[5] Biologists believed that enabling passage past the falls would provide many additional miles of spawning habitat and help stem the tide of declining numbers. These discussions came at the same time that plans for the Detroit Dam on the main stem North Santiam River were under way. Completed in 1953, the Detroit Dam blocked salmon from reaching 70 percent of their historic North Santiam spawning areas.[6] Fortunately, since the North Fork joins the full North Santiam down river from the dam, fish continue to have unobstructed passage into the North Fork watershed. This may have contributed to the interest in expanding spawning habitat along the North Fork.

By 1958, the Bureau of Commercial Fisheries (now the US Fish and Wildlife Service) had completed a fish ladder at Salmon Falls. Reports from 1958 indicate that the ladder was constructed by tunneling through the solid rock such that it would be hidden from public view, preserving the area's rustic aesthetic. As a boy, I walked on the massive rock above the falls with my dad when the men were working there. Only many years later could I appreciate what they did for the fish and the efforts they took to retain the natural beauty of the falls.

The fish counting device installed inside the ladder showed that the project was successful after only three years: hundreds of Chinooks and many more steelhead were able to reach new spawning areas upstream.[7]

In spite of the restoration efforts, fish numbers continued to drop so dramatically in the Willamette Basin that by 1999 the native (nonhatchery) winter steelhead and native spring Chinook in the upper basin were listed as threatened under the federal Endangered Species Act. The fish that had come to the North Fork for millions of years teetered on the edge of extinction.

Fish numbers have continued to decline in Oregon rivers because of a variety of human activities such as dams that block fish from spawning areas, loss of stream habitat, sediment from logging and agriculture, and other sources of pollution that reduce the oxygen needed by fish. Competition from nonnative hatchery fish, overfishing, and warming water connected to changing weather patterns have also contributed.[8]

Recent efforts to restore fish numbers throughout the Willamette Basin are pushing back against the decline. For instance, the Confederated Tribes of Grand Ronde purchased land in 2013 along the mainstem North Santiam River to enhance habitat for spring Chinook and winter steelhead, and other conservation values. Known by the tribes as the Chankawan, a Kalapuya word for salmon, the property is in the vicinity of the ancient Santiam Kalapuyan village of Anhalpum.[9] At about the same time, the Confederated Tribes of Siletz Indians also purchased lands in the watershed of the mainstem North Santiam River. They manage these lands to benefit fish and wildlife, as well as to conserve habitats that favor traditional foods such as camas, acorns, and wapato.

Along the North Fork, other projects are also making a difference. BLM is working on fish habitat projects on lands it manages. The nonprofit North Santiam Watershed Council is coordinating projects on private land along the river. Dad would have been pleased to know that the fish ladder continues to be maintained at Salmon Falls.

THINGS THAT ALMOST DID

Learning North Fork history has taught me that sometimes it's the things that don't happen over time that are as important to the story of a place as the things that do. Since the 1950s, three major developments almost happened—developments that, if implemented, would have changed the North Fork forever: a massive dam, a large real estate development, and an industrial-scale mine. Each project in its time came close to fruition, but all were eventually scrapped.

The (Almost) Lyons Dam

A regional study conducted in the 1960s by the Willamette Basin Task Force and the Pacific Northwest River Basins Commission suggested that the network of existing dams in the Willamette Basin might not be enough to prevent major winter flooding in the region. The study recommended another dam to be built—this one on the free-flowing North Fork. To be called the Lyons Dam, it was to stand 215 feet high (slightly taller than the immense Bonneville Dam on the Columbia River) and would create a reservoir behind it nearly 5 miles long and a mile wide. It would have filled all of Elkhorn Valley upstream to Salmon Falls, just short of our cabin property. The study spoke of providing "increased stream flows for water quality and downstream fishery enhancement, a reservoir fishery and water-oriented recreation" but did not refer to a fish ladder or any other way to enable wild fish to swim upstream past the dam. Instead of enhancing spawning habitat for wild fish runs, it would have further decreased existing habitat in Elkhorn Valley and eliminated access to the Salmon Falls fish ladder and habitat areas upstream.

Although the project was listed as "high priority," records are not clear as to why construction did not move forward. Possibly, projected costs were too high or the threat to fish populations too risky. Or planners may have realized that the proposal came while there was strong public support for designation of the North Fork as a State Scenic River. It is hard to fathom that recreation sites, homes, and cabins plus many miles of fish habitat could have been lost in the bottom of a deep reservoir.[10]

The Large-Scale Real Estate (Almost) Development

Some twenty years after the scrapped dam project, private developers planned an expansion of the nine-hole golf course in Elkhorn Valley and construction of 150 homes, 46 condominium units, and a commercial area.[11] Marion County approved the plan, but public opposition led to an appeal on grounds that it would overload the canyon's infrastructure and forever change the rural character of the North Fork. The appeal was rejected, and the golf course expansion finally went ahead in 2000, but the housing and commercial projects were never launched. As time passed, approval for the housing and commercial developments expired.

The Large-Scale (Almost) Mine

Salt Lake City–based Plexus Mining Company proposed a major copper mine in 1991 on national forest land in the Cedar Creek area of the upper canyon. The plan included hauling rock down North Fork Road on large trucks multiple times each day. Minibuses and trucks would make fifteen to twenty daily round trips to haul workers and supplies. Forest Service planners determined that traffic control on the roads might be needed. The Forest Service approved the proposal in principle, although more detailed plans and additional permits were still required before work could begin.

Members of the public opposed the plans on the argument that the mine would cause irreparable harm to the watershed and negatively affect irrigation and drinking water for downstream communities. Oregon's Department of Environmental Quality turned down the proposal, citing a rule prohibiting industrial discharge into the main North Santiam River. No permits were issued, and the mine was never developed.[12]

In the absence of these large-scale developments, lands in the lower canyon remained largely as they had been through the last half century. In the upper canyon, only narrow gravel roads and small mining operations penetrated the otherwise rugged and wild environment.

I can easily picture driving from Elkhorn into the national forest of the wild upper canyon on family trips during that era. As the canyon grew steeper and narrower with each mile, we approached the old wooden bridge over Henline Creek. Its well-worn steel treads made a "ker-plank, ker-plank" sound as we slowly crossed the river that roared far below and entered the enchanted place of giant trees, steep rocky cliffs, spectacular waterfalls, and seemingly impenetrable mountains. We passed the tiny Pearl Creek Guard Station, where several Forest Service cabins stood among the tall trees. As a boy, this compound intrigued me. It was even deeper in the mountains than our Elkhorn cabin.

We knew that James Hewitt and his Amalgamated Mines surrounding Jawbone Flats lay hidden just a few miles farther up the North Fork from Pearl Creek. Sometimes we read stories about his mines in the news, but because that part of the upper canyon was always closed to the public with a locked gate in those days, we often turned up a side road that followed the canyon of Cedar Creek, a tributary of the North Fork.

Along Cedar Creek, we always stopped at one of our favorite places in the canyon: a well-known roadside waterfall called Sullivan Falls, where a characteristic brown wooden Forest Service sign with yellow lettering announced our arrival. The narrow falls on Sullivan Creek dropped out of the forest over rocks high above the road before joining Cedar Creek. Sometimes when clouds hung low, the mesmerizing water seemed to drop out of the sky. Clear, cold, and emerald green, the water plunged into a round pool surrounded by western redcedar, sword fern, and vine maple. Because of its stunning beauty, the spot was sometimes written up in local papers, and we often took cabin guests to see it.

One summer day in 1971, my family and I traveled to visit the falls as we had done many times before. But this time, as we approached the falls, we barely recognized it; it looked like an explosion had torn the forest apart. The mountainside around the falls had just been logged. Where there had been towering cedars and Douglas-firs, Sullivan Creek now tumbled through stumps and broken wood debris. The parklike landscape was devastated—and so were we. Our family had long accepted logging as a fact of life in Oregon, including the North Fork, yet it was hard to understand why one of the best known and most beautiful spots in the North Fork canyon had to be logged right up to the falls. It became clear that logging had expanded into the upper canyon; as a young man, the experience had a big impact on me, and I found myself thinking about it long afterward.

Among many changes on the North Fork during my lifetime, the improved roads and bridges, electricity, and phone service were undoubtedly celebrated by many in the canyon. Other planned developments with potential to pollute the river, overwhelm canyon roads, and flood Elkhorn Valley were unwelcome among many others.

Logging operations were expanding into the wild upper reaches of the canyon at the same time that increasing numbers of people were coming to the North Fork for recreation. Many, including me, began to recognize the importance of conservation and protection of Oregon's special places. The parallel canyon stories of logging and conservation were about to collide.

14
Battle for Opal Creek

By the 1950s, even with developments reaching upriver into Elkhorn Valley and logging operations moving upstream along Cedar Creek, most of the Willamette National Forest lands of the upper canyon remained wild and undisturbed by human activities. Our family continued to make summer trips up the narrow road beyond Elkhorn, often stopping at Shady Cove, where Cedar Creek empties into the North Fork. Campers enjoyed a primitive campground there while hikers, berry pickers, hunters, and fishers found their way into even more remote areas nearby. Forests grew tall and, during the coming years, the area upstream along the North Fork from Shady Cove became known as one of the largest remaining unlogged tracts of old-growth forest in western Oregon. Some of the trees there were especially large, and pristine streams cascaded down from every mountain.

By the 1970s, Oregonians began to hear stories about the Opal Creek valley in the upper canyon of the North Fork through reports in newspapers, magazines, television, and radio reports—even a book and a movie. The battle for its future caught Oregon's attention—and put Opal Creek and the North Fork on the map.

A conflict had begun in the 1960s when the US Forest Service began planning for a new logging road into the upper North Fork canyon. It grew into an epic battle—a tug-of-war over the area's ancient trees and other attributes of the forested canyon. I had explored these mountains all through my young life and was approaching my twenties when the debate began. It attracted my attention—and my involvement.

The upper canyon's character remained largely as it had been a thousand years earlier. Its steep cliffs served as a kind of gate that restricted access and helped preserve the area as a true wilderness. But things were changing; Willamette National Forest managers sought to open the extensive pristine forests of the upper North Fork canyon for logging, including the removal of old-growth trees, some five hundred to eight hundred years old, along Opal Creek. Because the primitive mining road and old half-bridges were not suited for transporting modern logging equipment, engineers drew up plans for a major new road that would require blasting through the solid rock cliffs and bridging the deep side canyons.

Miner James Hewitt, proprietor of the Amalgamated Mining Company, didn't like the plan. Although there was little active mining there at the time, the new road would need to go through his claims and mining camp at Jawbone Flats. He didn't want people coming there, and without his cooperation, road construction could not move ahead.[1]

At about this time, in response to growing national interest in conservation and protection of natural landscapes, President Lyndon Johnson signed the 1964 National Wilderness Preservation Act, designed to protect some of America's last remaining wildlands. To qualify as designated wilderness, the act stipulated that an area must be free of human influence, offer "outstanding opportunities for solitude," and contain "ecological, geological, or other features of scientific, educational, scenic or historical value."[2] The Forest Service began a review of all remaining roadless lands within the national forests to determine their eligibility for possible future wilderness designation. The study became known as the Roadless Area Review and Evaluation, or RARE.

Wilderness advocates called special attention to the roadless area in the upper North Fork canyon that wrapped around three sides of Hewitt's mining enclave, called the Little North Santiam Roadless Area. They also pointed to a sizable area on the Mount Hood National Forest that shared a border with the North Fork called the Bull of the Woods Roadless Area, after a mountain in the area with that name. Believing that these roadless areas fully met the requirements in the new Wilderness Act, conservationists began calling for their protection as official wilderness areas.

Forest Service managers opposed wilderness designation of these areas. In 1971, road crews went to work surveying for the new road but soon found some of their survey markers pulled out, resulting in significant lost work. Suspecting that miners had removed the survey stakes, a state trooper and a Forest Service ranger traveled to the mines to confront the miners. The trooper and some of the miners were armed. Words were exchanged, and the officials departed. Within a few days, a larger group of law enforcement officers arrived at Jawbone Flats and took two miners into custody. After their release the following day, one of the men left the area, but the other—George Atiyeh—stayed on.[3]

Eight months later, James Hewitt died, leaving the mining claims to his daughter Delores and her husband, Vic Atiyeh (George Atiyeh's uncle and an influential state senator who later became Oregon governor). Vic enjoyed visiting the remote canyon, but neither he nor Delores had any interest in running the mining business and put the mines up for sale. In search of a buyer, their son Tom Atiyeh and his friend Rick Schaeffer introduced Hawaiʻi-based investors Thurston and David Twigg-Smith to the property. The Twigg-Smith brothers eventually purchased the mining properties and changed the name from Amalgamated Mines to Shiny Rock Mining Company. They appointed Tom Atiyeh as president and his cousin, George Atiyeh, as vice president. As Hewitt had done for years, the newly formed company continued to resist road construction and keep visitors out.[4]

By 1972, the Forest Service finished its RARE study that deemed the Little North Santiam Roadless Area and the Bull of the Woods Roadless Area eligible for designated wilderness consideration.[5] Soon after the study was released, a coalition of teachers, students, retirees, and trades professionals from Salem and nearby communities formed an organization called the Central Cascades Conservation Council (4 Cs) to advocate for conservation policies in western Oregon. The new group began advocating for designation of the two roadless areas as wilderness.[6]

By this time, I'd had time to reflect on my lifetime of experiences in the canyon and my emerging interests in conservation. Change was coming to the last unprotected wildland areas in western Oregon as road construction and logging reached deeper and deeper into nearly every canyon. The natural qualities of places like the North Fork were being lost. With the vast majority of forestlands in western Oregon already open for logging, I did not want to watch these last wild places disappear one by one. I feared that young people, including my own daughter, might not be able to grow up with opportunities for the same kind of meaningful wild-country experiences I had had. I joined the 4 Cs, adding my voice for conservation. It was a turning point for me. As one who admired the beauty and diversity of the natural world, I now began to speak out as an advocate for the wise stewardship of our nation's lands and natural resources.

Our group labeled the combined 50,000-acre Little North Santiam/ Bull of the Woods Roadless Area the "Hidden Wilderness," in part because the area was tucked between two well-known wilderness areas at Mount Hood and Mount Jefferson. We pointed to the North Fork's role as a source of municipal drinking water and praised its value for outdoor recreation close to Willamette Valley population centers. We asserted that the old-growth forests were some of the finest remaining in Oregon, providing habitat for several threatened wildlife species and serving as a laboratory for study of old-growth forests. Our group began communicating with Forest Service leaders and members of Congress about the proposal. We realized that to have the area designated as wilderness, the proposal would need to be shaped into legislative language, approved by both the US House and Senate, and signed into law by the president—a formidable set of hurdles. We knew we would need public support, and a lot of it.

The 4 Cs introduced the Hidden Wilderness proposal to Oregonians by producing a brochure titled *An Invitation to a Hidden Wilderness*, describing the area and touting its wilderness attributes. An important source of mass communication before the days of social media, the widely distributed publication encouraged readers to explore the area and write letters of support to the Forest Service.

Not everyone agreed with the proposed wilderness designation. Key Forest Service managers and timber industry representatives of the time believed the area should be reserved for timber management, including logging and reforestation, citing the importance of local timber jobs and community economic vitality.

In 1976, representatives of the Shiny Rock Mining Company and the 4 Cs arranged to meet about the wilderness proposal. It was an unlikely meeting, with two unconventional partners—representing mining and conservation. Tony George and John Brandt, founding members of the 4 Cs, and George Atiyeh from Shiny Rock met under a cedar tree at Jawbone Flats to discuss their common interests. Shiny Rock owners and managers wanted to retain the natural qualities of the area but also realized that, in order to protect it, they could no longer work to keep people out. Instead, as a strategy for increasing public support for wilderness designation, the three men agreed to work together to encourage visitors to explore the proposed wilderness area. From this point forward, members of the new coalition said they needed to "share it or lose it."[7]

The 4 Cs published *A Hiker's Guide to Oregon's Hidden Wilderness*, describing twenty-four trails in the area.[8] The group hosted public meetings and presented slide programs throughout the Willamette Valley. Council members met with Forest Service and congressional leaders and led hikes. Other conservation and outdoor recreation groups joined in support of the Hidden Wilderness proposal, including Friends of Bagby Hot Springs, Friends of Bull of the Woods, Chemeketans hiking club, Portland Advocates of Wilderness, and Oregon Wilderness Coalition.

Shiny Rock's George Atiyeh and 4 Cs members Vina Coffel and I traveled to Washington, DC, in 1977 to testify in support of the Hidden Wilderness and the Omnibus Wilderness bill sponsored by Oregon's Republican Senator Mark Hatfield. The timber industry also sent representatives, who advocated that the area should be opened for timber harvest to support local jobs and log supply for nearby lumber mills. At age twenty-four, I had never been to Washington, DC, and found myself in an ornate Senate hearing room, surrounded by the timber industry lobbyists. I remember feeling like David—the underdog—in the biblical story of a fight between the young David and a giant named Goliath.

Meeting in his office later that day, Senator Hatfield told us he was taking note of our proposal and the widening public support. He applauded our unusual alliance of conservationists and miners—two groups that often disagree on conservation issues.

Hatfield's final bill included three new wilderness areas in Oregon but did not include the Hidden Wilderness. Undeterred, supporters produced a public service video promoting protection of the area and wrote countless letters of support to newspapers, the Forest Service, and elected officials. George Atiyeh gave media interviews and, as a pilot, offered flights over the area to show people the undeveloped lands from the air. His passionate advocacy for protecting Opal Creek brought him statewide prominence.

Supporters argued that more than 90 percent of Oregon's forests were already available for logging and that some of the remaining wild forests, like the unique lands in the upper canyon of the North Fork, should be left undeveloped for the future. Further, Oregon contained a lower

Testifying at the US senate hearings in Washington, DC, in support of Senator Hatfield's Oregon Omnibus Wilderness bill, 1977. Myself (4 Cs) left, George Atiyeh (Shiny Rock Mining Co.) middle, and Vina Coffel (4 Cs) right. (*Photo courtesy of the US Senate Historical Office.*)

percentage of its public lands protected as wilderness than any of the surrounding states of Washington, Idaho, California, and Nevada.[9]

It was 1978, and I did not want to leave Oregon and the North Fork, but it was time to begin shaping my career. By this time my wife and I had a young daughter, and I had longed for professional work in conservation. When a position opened up in Idaho's Sawtooth National Forest—the best opportunity I'd seen—my friends and family promised to keep me informed on the wilderness debate if I applied. I accepted the job in the Wilderness Zone of the Sawtooth National Recreation Area while the debate over the Hidden Wilderness continued back in Oregon.

Three years after I left for Idaho, the Forest Service made new plans for a timber sale in the upper canyon near Opal Lake that would avert the need for a road through Jawbone Flats. Conservationists asserted that any proposed logging in the roadless area should be held off until a final decision about wilderness designation was made. A legal appeal brought by multiple conservation groups and individuals stopped the timber sale.[10] The debate was not always civil.

In early 1984, Oregon's US congressman Jim Weaver gained passage of the Oregon Wilderness Act that created the 35,000-acre Bull of the Woods Wilderness. It included all of the Bull of the Woods Roadless Area plus a portion of the Little North Santiam Roadless Area along Battle Ax Creek. While it represented a win for wilderness advocates, it was only a partial success because it left more than 15,000 acres of the Hidden Wilderness proposal (including the Opal Creek area) open to development. For some lawmakers, commercially valuable old-growth trees along Opal Creek and the remnants of primitive mining sites (indicating it had already been influenced by humans) made it unsuitable to include in the new wilderness bill.

Later that summer, the Forest Service held a dedication of the new Bull of the Woods Wilderness on the flank of Battle Ax mountain. By this time, I was working at Mount St. Helens, but I attended the dedication and celebrated the new wilderness area with many friends. Everyone acknowledged the future of the Opal Creek section was still an unsettled question.

A year after the dedication ceremony, 4 Cs's Tony George and Shiny Rock's Joseph Weber completed a book titled *The Santiam Mining District of the Oregon Cascades: A Cultural Property Inventory and Historical Survey.*[11] Documenting the area's rich mining history and Native American cultural significance, it led to a determination by the State of Oregon that the historic Jawbone Flats buildings and nearby bridges and half-bridges were eligible for nomination to the National Historic Register.[12] Eligibility for the registry carried an important new reality: no road could be built through the historic area at Jawbone Flats.

By 1988, the center of debate focused squarely on the unprotected Opal Creek drainage that was still roadless and trailless but still vulnerable to future development. To enable more people to see it, and support its protection, conservationists felt a trail was needed, but the Forest Service had no plans for building one. Curiously, a rough trail appeared in the Opal Creek canyon. George Atiyeh, Michael Donnelly, and several others knew all about the trail, but since a trail had not been approved by the Forest Service, the men said it must have been "built by bears." News writers picked up on the nickname Bear Trail and published stories describing the remarkable canyon—and hikers followed. A short time later, Tony George met with a local photographer to plan a poster that would publicize the threatened beauty of Opal Creek. Six conservation groups teamed up to produce the poster, featuring a stunning photograph with the label: "Opal Creek—Oregon's Uncut Gem."[13]

The Oregon State Legislature considered a bill to create an Opal Creek Ancient Forest State Park in 1989 and hearings were held in the capitol. Supporters said they were out "to protect a valuable and dwindling resource," while logging industry workers said they were out "to protect their jobs and the local economy." Nearly a hundred log trucks circled the capitol with horns honking in opposition. The bill failed, but extensive news coverage of the drama caught the attention of countless people in Oregon and across the United States—the Battle for Opal Creek became a national story.[14]

Just a year later, the US Fish and Wildlife Service listed the northern spotted owl as an endangered species. With spotted owls living along Opal Creek, the listing gave another justification for long-term wilderness protection.

The National Audubon Society produced a film called *Ancient Forests: Rage Over Trees,* continuing the widespread coverage of the story. Narrated by actor Paul Newman, it focused on the protracted battle over Opal Creek and was broadcast across the United States. Still more publicity came in 1993 when author David Seideman's book *Showdown at Opal Creek: The Battle for America's Last Wilderness* was published and distributed nationwide. The book focused on the conflict between longtime friends George Atiyeh and Tom Hirons, a local logger who sought to protect a way of life by opening areas like Opal Creek for logging.

By this time, wilderness advocates had formed a new group called Friends of Opal Creek. The group sought protection of the area and began to envision transforming the old Jawbone Flats mining camp into a conservation education center.

Oregon congressman Mike Kopetski championed yet another federal wilderness bill (the Opal Creek Forest Preserve Act of 1994), and it moved through the US House, but Senator Hatfield said there was not enough time to get the bill through the Senate during that session. He pledged to work on legislation in the next session.[15]

Hatfield kept his pledge. While he had long supported the timber industry in Oregon and recognized that timber was an important part of Oregon's economy, he was familiar with Opal Creek and its unique qualities; he had been hearing and talking about the area for twenty years. He knew the area was still wild and met all requirements for wilderness designation. He knew the ancient forests were ecologically important and hosted threatened wildlife species dependent on old-growth forests. He knew clean water from the canyon contributed to city water supplies, including the state capital of Salem. He knew of the old mining camp's historical and cultural significance and the area's unique recreation values for Oregon's growing population. Further, he understood there was a group of people dedicated to preserving the historic mining camp and using it for conservation education.

Senator Hatfield asked a group of conservationists, timber industry representatives, and public officials to work together to make recommendations for language to be used in Opal Creek Wilderness legislation. When the group formed, it proposed that eligible lands would be designated as wilderness while much of the remaining wildland in the headwaters of the North Fork containing evidence of the old mines, including the Shiny Rock claims and the historic mining camp at Jawbone Flats, would be designated as a Scenic Recreation Area. In addition, to help make up for timber revenues lost because of the designation, the legislation would provide $15 million in federal funding to support economic development in the Santiam Canyon. Senator Hatfield included this language in his Oregon Resource Conservation Act of 1996 and moved it through Congress.

Finally, in a high-stakes Washington, DC, budget meeting in September 1996, congressional leaders met to make final adjustments on their proposed federal budget. Senator Hatfield had placed his conservation legislation in the package; the meeting had gone on for hours, and it was past midnight. To avoid a government shutdown, all remaining changes needed to be finalized quickly. After 1:30 a.m., a last-minute motion was made to remove Senator Hatfield's Opal Creek legislation from the package. If the motion carried, protection for Opal Creek would yet again be passed over. But he had made a pledge to protect Opal Creek, and this was the retiring US senator's last opportunity to follow through on it. He addressed the group, insisting that his conservation legislation would be staying in the package. After consultation with others in the room, the House Speaker turned to Hatfield and said, "I think we have your message, and it stays."[16]

That was it. The Opal Creek legislation became part of a larger 1996 national bill including protection of additional lands in multiple states. Called the Omnibus Parks and Public Lands Management Act, it was signed into law by President Bill Clinton on November 12, 1996.

In the months that followed, significant work was needed to meet requirements of the legislation. Friends of Opal Creek transitioned to become a new nonprofit called the Opal Creek Ancient Forest Center and started designing a conservation education program.[17] The Shiny Rock Mining Company donated its claims in and around Jawbone Flats, valued at $12.5 million, to the new Ancient Forest Center. Microsoft cofounder Paul Allen donated $1.5 million for facility improvements for the education center.[18] Shiny Rock transferred ownership of all other mining claims to the Forest Service to become part of the Scenic Recreation Area, and workers cleaned up toxic mine tailings in the area. With this work completed, officials penned their signatures on November 9, 1998, finalizing the designation of the Opal Creek Wilderness (20,454 acres) and the Opal Creek Scenic Recreation Area (13,538 acres).[19]

Advocates for the protection of the upper North Fork and Opal Creek could have given up on their wilderness proposal numerous times when one bill after another failed to clear the hurdles of Congress. Instead, the charismatic activism of George Atiyeh and the strategic work of people like Tony George and Tom Atiyeh, combined with the behind-the-scenes work of many others, finally resulted in protection of the upper canyon. The epic twenty-year battle for Opal Creek was over.

A WALK IN THE OPAL CREEK WILDERNESS, JULY 2020

After researching North Fork history for more than five years, I made a midsummer trip with five companions into the wild country of the upper canyon. Our group entered the forest with backpacks and a sense of relief as we stepped away from daily routines. As we entered the Opal Creek Wilderness, tall white bear grass blooms marked our way, and the bright red of Indian paintbrush and spiked blooms of blue lupine greeted us around many turns. Sweet mountain air cooled us as it arced over the ridges where we walked.

Battle Ax Mountain and the Opal Creek Wilderness, July 2020. (*Photo by the author.*)

We crossed boulder fields of andesite that made music under our feet as rocks pitched back and forth, playing one against another. In every direction we looked across wild rugged canyons with no signs of roads or human development. To the west, Battle Ax Creek flowed down its glaciated canyon through evergreen forests toward Jawbone Flats. To the north lay the Bull of the Woods Wilderness, with its 2,000-acre silver forest, a stand of sun-bleached trees burned by the Mother Lode Fire in 2011. When clouds cleared, Mount Jefferson stood out like a giant pyramid, glazed with a finish of eternal snow.

One morning we awakened before dawn to the sound of owls calling to each other back and forth in the forest around us. Back on the trail, we passed beneath enormous trees and alongside younger trees growing among

charred stumps of forests burned by fires decades earlier. We walked along an ancient ridgetop trail and stopped to drink from a spring as we imagined travelers drinking from the same spring a thousand years ago.

On the last day of the trip, we set out to walk a section of the Forest Service trail that had not been maintained in some time, probably years. Our goal was to reach a particular view point. The trail was in good shape when we started but began to get rough. We struggled to climb over fallen trees toppled by winter storms and stepped carefully to avoid tripping on the tangled roots of trees and shrubs growing onto the trail. Six-foot-tall salmonberry bushes crowded us until our path became obscured. The hillsides became steeper and water began running in the trail, hidden by overhanging shrubs. One member of our group took a tumble, landing in the brush below. Others lent him a hand, and our group continued on. We stepped into ankle-deep mud as we picked our way through the tangle. Devil's club, a well-named shrub with long thorns, leaned punishingly into the trail.

At almost the same moment the route felt completely impassable, our way opened and we stepped out into the sunlight of a wide-open rocky mountainside. This was the destination and view point we had hoped to reach. We dropped our packs and looked out into the broad canyon below us.

As we stood together on that sunny July afternoon, Battle Ax—the old volcano—rose above us at the head of the North Fork canyon with a wild evergreen forest below and rocky ridges all around. This was the country I'd known all my life and here it was, still wild, just as it was when I was young—now part of the Opal Creek Wilderness.

15
Beachie Creek Fire, 2020: The Fire Wasn't Supposed to Do This

It was three weeks after the Beachie Creek fire burned along the North Fork that my daughter and I made our first trip back into the canyon, finding the landscape dramatically changed. There were times that day we barely recognized this canyon we had known for so long. Although we had carefully read all the daily fire reports up to that time, more detailed news reports and stories surrounding the fire were only beginning to be told.

As the weeks and months passed, I read more about the megafire, spoke with firefighters who were on duty the day it exploded and with local residents who came face-to-face with the fire during the night that followed. Gradually, details about the fire and the experiences of people in its path began to emerge.

Positioned high on French Creek Ridge above Opal Lake, US Forest Service fire operations chief John Spencer had monitored the warm and dry conditions on that Labor Day morning, aware of the east wind predicted for later in the day. John later told me, "It was a calm morning with benign fire activity through mid-day" and he could see the fire as it slowly burned in the basin below him. He could see helicopters dropping buckets of water on the fire through the day, keeping it in check.

As small gusts of wind arrived in midafternoon, John recalled, "the tops of trees started moving and leaves started rattling. At first, gusts came in small pulses, with periods of calm in between. When the stronger gusts started hitting the fire, everything began to change."

Waves of wind hit the forest and several large trees burst into flames. Smoke started rising up from clusters of burning trees, forming a fire front. That's when—as John describes—"the fire stood up." It was 3:05

p.m. "The fire began to make deep rumbling noises like passing trains, followed by a big column of black smoke." The fire made a run, engulfing trees as it climbed out of the basin toward the crest of French Creek Ridge where John and his crew were working. As winds increased, enormous trees torched, sending flames 100 feet into the air.

It was unsafe to stay any longer. John and his crew received orders to clear out; there was nothing more they could do to hold the fire from spreading. The crew made it safely to fire camp in Gates. John was the last one to leave the ridgetop.[1]

A few miles north, Oregon Department of Forestry (ODF) personnel Eric Perkins and Spencer Mitchell wrapped up at the Ancient Forest Center at Jawbone Flats where they had been working for several days fire-hardening the site. They set sprinklers, trimmed trees, and mowed grass in case the fire should threaten there (while the US Forest Service was responsible for fighting the fire itself, ODF had responsibility for protecting private property near the fire). Around 5 p.m., unaware that winds had started on the high ridges, the two men headed down toward the ODF headquarters in Mehama for what was typically a one-hour drive.

The winds rose quickly, and the pair arrived at what became the first of many downed trees blocking the road. It took only a few minutes to cut and move the first tree, but each mile brought more limbs and larger windthrown trees. Travel through the increasing smoke was slow. As darkness began to fall, a bright orange glow from the fire rose behind them in the east. Just as they reached Elkhorn Valley—still some 10 miles from the forestry office and still out of cell and radio range—they came upon multiple crisscrossed trees on the road that had become entangled with downed electrical lines.

In total darkness and with headlights trained on the down trees, the two firefighters surveyed their situation with deep concern. How could they safely remove the trees from this tangled mess? They had planned to be back at headquarters long ago, and managers would be concerned. They knew they could get the trees cleared, but if one of them got hurt they could be faced with an even more dire situation.

Avoiding power lines and flying debris, they began sawing. They had just finished clearing a path through the jumble when a welcome pair of headlights appeared on the other side of the downed trees. Coworkers Don Everingham and Scott West had driven up the canyon to look for them. Relieved to see Eric and Spencer, Don assured them that North Fork Road below this point was all clear. They agreed that Eric and Spencer would load their chainsaw and make the remaining twenty-minute trip back to headquarters while Don and Scott would head out of the canyon over Gates Hill for their next assignment.[2]

A few minutes after Don and Scott left, Eric and Spencer resumed their trip down North Fork Road but found another tree across the road in the short time since Don and Scott passed through. The two jumped out of the truck and cut it, but drove only a short distance before they found even more trees blocking the road. The winds were now howling. The men noticed glowing embers flying horizontally above their heads.

By this time, Eric estimated the wind was roaring a steady 50 mph, with gusts of 70 mph or more through the trees. To communicate, they had to shout even when standing close together. With each gust, they could hear large trees crashing to the ground, some very close to the truck. More than once, they dove for safety.

Soon they came to an enormous tree blocking the road, much larger than others they had cleared. This one was suspended above the road, like an overpass, but was too low to drive under and there was no way around it. An experienced sawyer, Spencer began cutting the tree into segments while Eric wrapped a chain around the pieces and dragged them off the road with the truck. They knew they had to be extremely careful with the saw: if they got it bound up, they had no other saw. After nearly thirty minutes, the men finally drove past the tree. The work had challenged their skills, endurance, and emotions; they couldn't help but wonder if they were going to make it out. No one had understood how much worse the conditions would get.

At the next downed tree in the road, another set of headlights appeared—this time from behind. It was a vehicle of North Fork residents evacuating the canyon. The car had been driving through the openings Eric and Spencer had cut along the road. A man jumped out and helped pull debris from the roadway. The two vehicles drove in tandem a short distance to another downed tree. They teamed up to remove it as two more cars pulled up behind them—more evacuees and more help. More cars joined the line.

The caravan finally made it safely to the Santiam Highway. North Fork residents dispersed toward Salem while Eric and Spencer pulled into the parking lot at the ODF fire headquarters. The drive from Jawbone Flats had taken nearly six hours.

Don and Scott made it back to headquarters at about the same time. As the four men reunited, Don shared their story. He and Scott had successfully driven over Gates Hill and radioed headquarters to report that Eric and Spencer were safe. In the call they learned there were campers with horses at a campground south of Gates who may not know of the impending danger. Don and Scott had immediately turned their truck around and headed for the campground.[3]

As they drove, they could see fires burning and people evacuating. Despite the chaos, they pushed on toward the campground. Trees and debris littered the road, and they had to stop numerous times to clear the way. Arriving at the campground, they found the campers were indeed unaware of the rapidly approaching fire. The campers hastily loaded their horses and followed Don and Scott through the thick smoke toward Gates. Back on the highway, the camper's truck and horse trailer disappeared westward into the smoke safely toward Salem. Don and Scott made their way back toward headquarters in Mehama where they were urgently needed elsewhere.

On the drive back to the forestry office, Don observed, "flames rose on both sides of the Santiam Highway with fields and forests burning everywhere." He told me he worried about how bad things might get. Only the day before, he had seen computer models predict that the fire would not likely leave the high mountains. As he drove through the fire that night, he recalled thinking, "the fire wasn't supposed to do this."

Through the night, while most people in Santiam country evacuated, some stayed behind to help others and protect buildings. Back in Gates, the Forest Service fire camp caught fire when a power line came down in the strong winds. Firefighters there barely escaped, stomping out flames as they hurried to their trucks.

Recognizing the developing emergency, Ken Cartwright, general manager for KYAC community radio station in Mill City, left his Gates home around 10 p.m. after helping his wife evacuate down the canyon. He headed for the radio station to see if he could broadcast information about the emergency.[4] A retired navy radio man, he knew how to deal with SOS situations. He told me, "It was like Armageddon with fire on the mountainsides, sirens blaring, and people shouting in the streets." When electrical lines fell in the strong winds and power went out in Mill City, Ken needed to use the radio station's backup generator, but the generator's battery was dead, so he jump-started it with his truck. For the next four hours, he broadcast the "Go Now" evacuation orders for anyone who could still pick up his broadcast. He held his CB radio in one hand, gathering fire and road updates from other local CB users. In his other hand, he held the radio station's microphone to broadcast the latest available information on which roads were still passable for evacuation and which were blocked. At 2 a.m., the state police told him emphatically it was time for him to also leave. As he evacuated and reunited with his wife in Stayton, their home in Gates burned. By 3 a.m., the fire reached the Department of Forestry office in Mehama and burned it to ashes.

In just twelve hours, the fire had exploded, burning 130,000 acres of forest including the entire length of the North Fork canyon from Opal Lake to Mehama—many times larger than the area predicted by computer models.[5] The courageous actions of local volunteers and fire fighters likely saved lives that night. Some have been honored as heroes, while the work of many others has never become widely known. In many cases, people didn't get to thank those that helped save their lives and sometimes didn't even know who they were.[6]

Not everyone in the North Fork canyon had been aware of the rapidly emerging danger, leaving them little or no time to gather valuables and forcing them to find ways to escape or survive the fire on their own. Elkhorn Valley resident Don Myron told me he was at home sometime after 9 p.m. when he noticed tree limbs hitting his roof and went outside to investigate. Seeing fire on the mountains above him, he quickly grabbed a few personal things and tried to drive out. Unfortunately, a tree had fallen across North Fork Road near his home, too large to move. Realizing he had no way to proceed down canyon, he took shelter in the water of the North Fork beneath a nearby bridge. As fire encircled him, he sat on a large rock in the middle of the river, batting burning embers through the night with a plastic lawn chair he found beside the river. After a long night, Don made it safely out of the canyon the next day with help from search and rescue teams. Like his neighbors, he lost his home.[7]

Farther down canyon, near Lomkers Bridge, Scott Torgeson had returned home from a long kayaking trip late in the afternoon on Labor Day. Exhausted and unaware of the potential for the fire to approach his

Beachie Creek Fire burning along the banks of the North Fork in Elkhorn Valley. Don Myron survived the fire, finding refuge on a rock in the middle of the river. He snapped this photo at about 11 p.m. on September 7, 2020. (*Photo courtesy of Don Myron.*)

home, he decided to call it a day and get some sleep. At about midnight, a loud explosion awakened him, and he got up to see what had happened. When he opened the door, he saw his deck on fire and a neighbor's home burning. Grabbing keys and a few things from the table, he ran to his car as his house caught fire.

As he raced down the road in the blinding smoke, he hit a fallen tree and the car became high-centered with no way to free it. Knowing he couldn't go back to the house, and fearing the smoke by the river might be deadly, he decided to make a run for it down the road. Using his t-shirt as a mask, he alternately ran and walked. He estimates winds blew 60 to 70 mph as the fire burned on the mountainsides around him. He came upon a woman in distress unable to walk. They agreed he should continue down the road to a spot where he would have cell service and call 911 for help.

Continuing along the road he watched as a "fire ball" came up from the river in front of him, engulfing the road. The fire was all around him now, with the entire shoreline of the river burning and the road blocked by a wall of flames. Assessing his options, he saw no good choices. Covering his face and head as best he could, he ran forward and jumped through the wall of flames. To his amazement, he tumbled out the other side of the flames. He had made it, and the road ahead was free of fire as far ahead as he could see. Unaware of how badly he was burned, he continued along the road until he saw headlights approaching in the thick smoke. The driver said he was on his way up the road to find his wife. Scott realized the man's wife was the woman he had encountered and told him where she was. The man said he'd go get her and pick up Scott on the way out. Within a short time, the truck came back: the man had found his wife. The man made room for Scott in his vehicle and drove the three out of the canyon to safety. After telling me his story, Scott said, "That man is a hero, driving into the fire to save his wife and then stopping again to pick me up and drive us all out to safety."[8]

Sadly, others were not as fortunate. Five people lost their lives along the North Fork that night, unable to evacuate ahead of the fire. Theirs are the most tragic stories of the Beachie Creek Fire. Among them was George Atiyeh, well known for his decades of work to protect Opal Creek. He was at his Elkhorn Valley home when the fire came.

The stories of that terrifying night reveal the ferocity of the fire and the winds that blew through the canyons and carried the fire through the darkness. John Spencer had thirty-six years of firefighting experience, including twenty-one years as a smoke-jumper (among the most demanding firefighting jobs) and had worked on many horrific fires. Yet he said, "Seeing its [Beachie Creek Fire] speed and the way it burned through large west Cascades timber boggled my mind. I'd never seen anything like it."[9]

In a few parts of the lower canyon, the fire burned in a mosaic pattern, leaving patches of unburned forest, including near the golf course. But elsewhere, including Elkhorn with its forty homes, as well as the Opal Creek Scenic Area and Opal Creek Wilderness, little was spared. In heavily burned areas, fire burned plants and shrubs completely, sparing only their roots deep in the ground. In places the fire burned through the organic soil layers, leaving only rock, mineral soil, and ash. A forester working on

Blown-down trees along the North Fork, the result of hurricane-force winds the night of the fire. (*Photo by the author.*)

lands adjacent to our place estimated that a foot of organic material and topsoil was lost near our cabin. The forests that took centuries to grow burned in just a few hours.

Thousands of trees blew to the ground in areas subjected to the most powerful winds. In some places, winds blew so hard that every tree in areas the size of football fields uprooted or splintered and crashed to the ground. At times, the effects of that night have been overwhelming, and I've had to avert my eyes from the vastness of change.

The Beachie Creek Fire burned more than 193,000 acres, twice the size of what is classified as a mega-fire—and, further, it merged with another megafire (the Lionshead Fire) to make a footprint of almost 400,000 acres. The North Fork was in the center of the blaze, where it appeared to burn the most intensely. Ninety-four percent of the North Fork Watershed burned.[10]

Across western Oregon, three other mega-fires burned that night. No other single year in Oregon's recorded history had witnessed more than one mega-fire. In total, fires burned more than a million acres in western Oregon that weekend.[11]

Within a few months, land managers and the state transportation agency started cutting countless blackened but still-standing dead trees. Fire-killed trees still contained valuable wood fiber, and mill operators warned that within two years they would become prey to insects and disease. In addition, because dead trees along roadways were expected to become a hazard to motorists, wide swathes of forest were removed on either side of roads. We watched truckloads of scorched trees leave the canyon month after month. Each logging truck full of blackened canyon logs was a stark reminder of how much was changing in Santiam country.[12]

Discussions soon focused on forest management policies. Many forest ecologists believe that aggressive fire suppression during the past hundred years has increased fire hazards by allowing a buildup of dead wood and undergrowth in the forests, contributing to the intensity of fires. Within the timber industry, many argue there should be more logging to reduce this fuel buildup, while forest ecologists and others suggest there should be more managed fire to reduce the fuels and help reestablish fire-resilient forests.

When it came time to cut the fire-killed trees surrounding our cabin, I contracted with a local logger whose family had been logging in the area for four generations. He and I welcomed opportunities to talk about the fire, logging, reforestation and how to best manage our forests to be more fire-resilient. We agreed on some topics and disagreed on others; there will always be different ideas on how best to do things. Yet we agreed it was important to talk about our ideas and to also listen to what the other person is thinking. When he completed my job, he told me, "We're both environmentalists. We both want to have healthy forests and clean water for our kids, the way the forests were when we were young." We agreed to keep in touch—and we have.

Fires have burned in Oregon's Cascade mountain forests for thousands of years. Giant old stumps with black burn scars stood in North Fork forests all through my life, and in recent years I watched several fires burn in and near the North Fork canyon. Considering the recurring episodes of fire in these forests, it was no surprise that fire came again. From one perspective, the Beachie Creek Fire was part of the ongoing cycle through which forests have grown, burned, and regrown countless times through centuries past, where things are in continual flux and are always being transformed.

But things are shifting now. Records show Oregon's temperatures have been slowly rising for decades, and much of Oregon has been slipping in and out of drought in recent years. Climate scientist Larry O'Neill from Oregon State University says, "As the climate warms, the atmosphere increases its capacity to evaporate water not only from the soil but other things as well, so the drying trend will continue." He says there will still be periods of wet and dry, but the dry periods will be much more intense. O'Neill goes on to say, "What we saw in 2020 is a precursor for what we can expect in the future." He and other climatologists say it's not a matter of if, but when and where the next large fires will burn.[13]

I'm troubled by the thought that the Beachie Creek Fire may be a harbinger of things to come. It seems we are all in this together, and everyone shares in the responsibility to help find ways to make Oregon's forests and communities more fire-resilient as we face the reality that, as in the past, more fires will come.

The experience of the fire was unspeakably difficult for people along the North Fork. Those who lost family members or friends were left to grieve. People who sustained burns and other injuries have faced months and years of healing and rehabilitation. Many lost their homes and virtually all their possessions, some lost their places of business, while others, like our family, lost cherished family cabins.

In many cases, people faced financial hardships when home insurance coverage did not cover the rapidly rising costs of rebuilding. Families and timber companies took big economic losses as their trees burned. Some were still facing health challenges from the COVID-19 pandemic when the fire came. Others felt emotional strain from losing their homes and being scattered to temporary housing in distant towns.

Some homes and cabins lost were historic structures that many people had come to know and love. Among those were the Elkhorn Guest Ranch and Mrs. Wheeler's former home. Located in the heart of the firestorm, these landmark homes didn't stand a chance.

Just down river from Elkhorn, the fire took Lou and Laura Meyers's former home that had become known in recent years as the Elkhorn Valley Inn. The Cranberry House that encompassed the old Elkhorn School burned. Farther downriver, Governor Sprague's Thetford Lodge and the old Oakdale School were taken. All of the historic mining cabins and community buildings at the Ancient Forest Center burned; only one newer cabin at Jawbone Flats survived. With hardly an exception, all the historic buildings I have ever known in the North Fork canyon were taken by the Beachie Creek Fire.

Fire took the classic wood "ker-plank" bridge over Henline Creek. The steel treads that lined the bridge scattered along the creek far below. The fire took the old half-bridges along the way to Jawbone Flats and the old CCC-built Guard Station at Pearl Creek.

The fire brought some form of hardship, grief, and loss to everyone along the North Fork, as well as in other western Oregon communities. A longtime friend and neighbor at Elkhorn told me about when he and his wife made their first trip back up the canyon after the fire. He said, "We were in tears before we got five miles up the North Fork." I think we all felt the same way.

In the face of so much change, I regularly found myself thinking back to what things were like before the fire—and about what all was lost. Yet, as those first few years passed, I found myself increasingly focused on the canyon the way it is now.

Through the postfire challenges, I've also thought back to experiences in my career. I am encouraged by the memory of the surprising return of life to the landscape immediately following the Mount St. Helens eruption. From my years in Hawai'i, I have thought about the strength of islanders to rebuild their lives after lava flows overtook their homes and communities. From my years on the Tillamook State Forest, I have recalled the emotional story of the forest turning green again following the Tillamook Burn. Even within the grief and hurt following the Beachie Creek fire, I've had confidence that a story of rebirth would arise here along the North Fork too.

16
Beautiful Stream

Spring 2021 appeared along the North Fork as the cold dark days of winter gave way to sun and warmth. Even as canyon residents struggled with loss, many people coming up the canyon took note as life began to reappear across the landscape.

Green shoots sprouted from the deep roots of maple, dogwood, and cascara trees. Oregon grape and salal also poked up from the barren soil where their roots had survived the fire. Although evergreen trees in the Cascade Range don't resprout from roots, their vibrant green

Vegetation sprouting from a burned stump, spring 2021. (*Photo by the author.*)

1-inch-tall seedlings began sprouting from seed in the ash-covered ground. As instantly as fire had consumed the canyon's towering forests, life emerged again with barely a pause.

Even as my family and I dealt with our own challenges after the fire, we delighted in seeing what new plants and animals appeared on our trips up the canyon. We spotted larkspur and camas flowers along the roadsides, more prolific than before. It was still a blackened landscape, but life was appearing everywhere.

Swallows, hummingbirds, and quail returned. Ospreys and bald eagles fished the river. We saw deer, black bears, beaver—and even a cougar. We started seeing herds of elk, more than we'd ever seen in the canyon before. The return of plants and animals carried a promise of renewal, not only for the new forest, but for each of us affected by the fire.

Support for victims came quickly and from many sources. Twenty-two churches opened their doors to those who had lost their homes. The local Elks Club provided free breakfasts. The Red Cross came, giving out rakes, shovels, and gloves to victims. A quilter's guild gathered hundreds of colorful handmade quilts from across the United States and around the world as gifts for families who lost homes and cabins.[1] A few weeks after the fire, a local folk music group played a benefit concert that raised $10,000 for fire victims.

The North Santiam Watershed Council offered free native plants and tree planters to stabilize stream banks and curb soil erosion. A group established a tool lending library. Volunteers built and delivered free storage sheds, and the county waived building permit fees for those who'd lost homes and cabins.

In the months that followed, a local fire recovery nonprofit formed and raised millions of dollars to assist fire victims. In the aftermath of the fire, Congress approved the long-awaited $15 million promised through the Opal Creek Wilderness

Label sewn on one of the dozens of quilts gifted to fire victims after the fire from quilters across the country and around the world. (*Photo by the author.*)

legislation for economic development in the North Santiam canyon, including the North Fork.[2]

Some neighbors have expressed optimism as they've watched the new forest begin to rise and carpenters frame the first new houses. New homes and cabins began appearing in the canyon, including one belonging to our neighbor Denise, who summed it up: "I'm gonna be resilient, like the forest." Even though so much had changed, another neighbor looked me in the eyes and said, "It's good to be home."

My family and I agreed early on we would rebuild. The canyon was too much a part of our lives to consider anything else. As we drafted plans, we specified fire-resistant roofing, siding, glass, and venting. We committed to managing vegetation surrounding the new cabin to make it more defensible against future fires. We embraced the idea that our new place would be more like a cabin in a meadow than a cabin in the deep woods, much like the old homestead cabins built in clearings 150 years earlier.

After studying canyon history for so many years, I felt a monumental loss when the fire consumed most of the canyon's historic landmarks, including the oldest homes, cabins, and bridges. Yet as time passed and despite the loss of these historic structures, I realized many other elements of canyon history live on.

Countless pieces of obsidian and jasper, hidden for hundreds and thousands of years, will have survived this latest fire as they have withstood burns in centuries past. Left behind by ancient tool-makers, they will provide a link to the legacy of Native American life along this river since time before memory.

Even though all the cabins and community buildings from the 1920s and 1930s burned at Jawbone Flats, evidence of mining history remains in the form of rusty antique trucks and ore-carts that withstood the fire.

On some properties, old apple trees survived the fire and will continue to offer a living link to the early homesteads. The old Garford truck will live on, likely in a museum, where its stories from the early days of logging along the North Fork will continue to be told.

Even at our place, the original 1940s gravity tank has been refurbished and plumbed into our new water system as we finished rebuilding. We hope our grandchildren will point to reminders of the old cabin in the future as they tell stories about our family experiences in years past. I

understand more than ever what the Bickett sisters shared: "After you get to know a place, it's no longer just a place. It becomes a part of you."

People throughout North Fork history—from the Kalapuyas and Molallas to those who experienced the 2020 fires—have many things in common. They showed resilience in the face of challenging times. They teach us the importance of working together and supporting each other. In the Battle for Opal Creek, the unusual alliance of miners and conservationists illustrates the power of finding common ground with those who are often viewed as adversaries. Collectively, our stories are important to remember in days ahead, when difficult times come again.

The North Fork's conservation legacy will live on too, in the stories of John Breckenridge Waldo, the Tree Army Boys, the Cloud Girls, and Charles Sprague. Construction of the fish ladder at Salmon Falls, protection of Opal Creek, and the decision not to build the Lyons Dam will long be remembered as examples of how Oregonians chose to look after the land by protecting ecological, cultural, and recreational resources in the North Fork canyon.

Logging continues to have its place along the North Fork too, as it has for more than a hundred years. Policies guiding forestry practices in Oregon have evolved—and will continue to evolve—with the goal of protecting water, wildlife, and forest health into the future.

Resilient in the wake of the fire, the Opal Creek Ancient Forest Center continues to offer conservation education at alternative sites across Oregon while the staff explores opportunities for programs and facilities in the new environment. The conservation legacy that helped shape the North Fork canyon offers inspiration for navigating environmental challenges in the years ahead.

As I searched libraries and museums, attended history summits, and met with locals, I learned about places I'd never known about. Now I can travel to all these places in my mind, imagining what it might have been like to visit them many years ago. After learning so much about people from the past, I sometimes feel I've met them and known them myself.

My new awareness of area history has created a far richer and more meaningful appreciation for the canyon than I ever had before. I've heard

Facing page: I painted the old water tank that was the only thing at our cabin still standing after the fire, July 2021. (*Photo by Shawn Morford.*)

tribal members say that cultural history gives richness of understanding, like adding color to a black-and-white photo. My roots have grown even deeper into these volcanic rocks and soils than they were before.

I sometimes feel like the young boy lifted up by his father in the old sawmill to see things in a new light. I now see North Fork history as far more than a jumble of obscure facts that few people remember or care about anymore. Instead, I have come to recognize that within the long scope of North Fork history, there are timeless stories that teach us valuable lessons about life, if we will only listen.

I still spend a lot of time along the North Fork. More than ever, I feel deep gratitude for my lifetime of experiences there. Although so much has changed, I'm still drawn to the canyon. The surrounding mountains, no longer hidden by the dense forest, call out to me just as they did when I was a boy. Watching the plants of the forest resprout excites me, and I welcome their lessons of resilience as I continue to manage my health issues. I'll still be exploring the old trails, casting a fly in my favorite pools and, like Marion Taylor, just enjoying a spell in the outdoors.

One thing that has not changed in the canyon since the fire is that beautiful stream—the Little North Santiam River. It flowed from the mountains as they formed millennia ago and cut through them as the mountains grew higher. It nurtured the early forests, the Native people, the miners, and the homesteaders who followed. More recently it provided a place for recreation and renewal from a busy world. It offered shelter during the night of fire, and it continues to gift us with its presence.

The river still speaks with the sound of cascading waters. Its emerald green color captivates in the same way it always has; when sunlight touches it in the early morning, it reflects golden light up to the mountains like it has since the beginning of time.

Oh, have you not heard of that beautiful stream
That flows through our Father's land?
Its waters gleam bright in the heavenly light
And ripple o'er golden sand.

Golden sunrise along the North Fork, summer 2021. (*Photo by the author.*)

Acknowledgments

As I set out to learn Little North Santiam history, many people stepped up to assist me, sharing their knowledge, experiences, and stories. Without the help of this wide-ranging group, the writing of *Beautiful Stream* would not have been possible.

My understanding of canyon geology developed in large part from interviews with geologist David Sherrod and hydrologist Steve Sobieszczyk, both with the US Geological Survey.

Native American history within the Willamette Valley and the North Fork opened for me through conversations with Siletz tribal member Robert Kentta. My understanding grew through meetings with tribal members at Grand Ronde, beginning with Eirik Thorsgard, Misty Thorsgard, and David Harrelson and continuing with Stephanie Craig, Don Day, Bob Culbertson, Bobby Mercier, and Dr. David Lewis. US Forest Service archaeologists Tony Farque, Cara Kelly, and Cathy Lindburg, along with Oregon State Parks archaeologist Nancy Nelson, shared elements of history with me and helped identify people and documents that added to my learning.

From my earliest days of research, numerous individuals at the North Santiam Historical Society in Mill City championed my work as I researched everything from mining to logging and homesteading. Among them, Francis (Thomas) McGuire, Bev Redding, Carol Cree, Cindy Budlong, and Melody Munger gave special support.

Tony George shared his extensive knowledge of the early years of mining in the upper canyon, while George Atiyeh and Tom Atiyeh told me stories about their family's history at the North Fork mines. Dr. Bob Reinhardt and Norma Pennington unearthed remarkable stories from the mining era.

Terry Gookin, Steve Gookin, Al Ketchum, Bob Freres, and Dennis Frank, along with Dale and Gordon Kirsch, all helped me learn about the early days of North Fork logging.

Neighbors and friends all along the North Fork welcomed my research, sharing their knowledge of earlier years in the canyon. Craig Z. Randall and his sons Craig V. Randall and Kerry Randall told stories about the Elkhorn Guest Ranch. Steve Mitchell, Nancy Green, and Carl Pope shared their family stories from Elkhorn. Iva VanBeek, Bob Culbertson, and Pastor Troy Gulstrom shared their knowledge of early Mehama. Jo and Steve Philippi, Alice Bickett, Phyllis Fencl, Randall Tinney, Liz Cutler, Peter Scriven, and Todd Mobley all met with me to tell their canyon stories, while Bill Heuller, unable to meet in person during the 2020 COVID-19 era, shared his family stories through long conversations over the phone.

Journalist Floyd McKay revealed the conservation legacy of Oregon Governor Charles Sprague. Darrin Neff, fisheries biologist with the US Forest Service, helped me to better understand the river's native fish runs.

Through interviews with Tom Imeson, George Atiyeh, Tom Atiyeh, Rick Schaeffer, Mark Otenad, Tony George, John Brandt, Bob Pendledon, Ross Miller, Joe Walicki, Andy Kerr, James Montieth, and others, I relived the battle for Opal Creek while also learning new details from that time.

Librarians at the Oregon State Library, the Mark O. Hatfield Library at Willamette University, and municipal libraries in Salem, Stayton, and Lyons all helped me locate important references.

Staff and volunteers at museums throughout the Willamette Valley shared their knowledge. Alan Maul at the Oregon Department of Forestry's Forest History Center in Salem, Kylee Pine at the Mission Mill Museum in Salem, Ted Shepard at the Aumsville Historical Society, Diana Maul at Yesterday in Turner, Susan Masse at the Santiam Historical Society in Stayton, Bill Stoddard at Silver Falls State Park, Jack Hande at the Silverton Historical Society, and Rick Simmons at the Powerland Heritage Park in Salem were especially helpful. Staff at the Oregon Historical Society in Portland provided valuable assistance, as did others at the Chachalu Museum and Cultural Center in Grand Ronde, the Champoeg State Park Visitor Center, the Museum at Warm Springs, and the Peabody Museum of Archaeology and Ethnology at Harvard University. Volunteers at the Linn County Historical Museum in Brownsville, the

Museum of the Oregon Territory in Oregon City, the Museum of Natural and Cultural History in Eugene, and the Champoeg State Park Visitor Center all shared information.

From the early days of this project, historian and friend Doug Decker and environmental writer Edward (Ted) Wolf encouraged me and offered valuable inspiration. As I worked on early drafts of the book, Carol Cree, Marv and Barb Hawes, Lee Quiring, and others read the manuscript and gave valuable comments.

Following the Beachie Creek Fire, John Spencer, Don Everingham, Eric Perkins, Scott Torgeson, Don Myron, Ken Cartwright, Denise Collins, Paul Toews, Dave Warnack, Mike Messier, and Gabe Silbernagel shared stories about the fire, logging, tree planting, and rebuilding homes. Nathan Reynolds, Augustus (Auggie) Gleason, and Adam Mims shared about their work to rebuild the conservation education program at Opal Creek.

My brother John Quiring, my daughter Rachael Boehm, and my longtime friend Gene Rempel supported my research from the beginning. As I neared completion of the book, Zach Urness (*Statesman Journal*) and Michelle King (US Forest Service) helped locate photos. Heather Moore, photo historian at the US Senate Historical Office clarified key questions for me, and Andy Adkins created maps for the book.

At OSU Press, reviewers offered valuable comments, and Kim Hogeland guided me as I submitted the manuscript. Everyone at OSU Press was extremely helpful as we worked together to prepare the book for publication.

The greatest support throughout my work on this book came from my partner, Shawn Morford. Encouraging me, reading the evolving manuscript and offering comments, she was always there to back me up. As I wrapped up the project, she helped with proofreading, inserting endnotes, and assembling the bibliography—not small tasks. Her support was invaluable.

Since I began work on this project, more than twenty of the local people I interviewed have passed on. I am grateful for the opportunity to have met each of them, and to have learned North Fork history from them and captured their personal stories.

Looking back on my twelve years of learning, I deeply appreciate all these individuals—and others—who have shared knowledge of North

Fork history and supported my work along the way. My life is richer because of them and I am indebted to them all.

I have made every effort to describe this history accurately and fairly, based on my research. I welcome corrections for future editions.

Notes

Prologue

1 US Department of Agriculture, Forest Service, "2020 Beachie Creek Fire Storymap—Chapter 1." The US Forest Service describes the origin of the fire, its first three days of growth, and agency's efforts to suppress it. Photographs and interactive maps help portray the story. Also see US Department of Agriculture, Forest Service, "Beachie Creek Fire" (overview).
2 US Department of Agriculture, Forest Service, "2020 Beachie Creek Fire Storymap—Chapter 2." Chapter 2 outlines the increasing fire danger, gradual growth of the fire, and agency efforts to contain it in late August and early September. Also see US Department of Agriculture, Forest Service, "Beachie Creek Fire" (overview).
3 National Weather Service, "Beachie Creek Fire, Northwest Oregon." This National Weather Service website chronicles the concerns that grew day by day for a major wind event in early September.
4 National Weather Service, "Beachie Creek Fire, Northwest Oregon."
5 Urness, "Oregon Wildfires."
6 Urness, "Oregon Wildfires."
7 "Oregon's Air Is So Hazardous It's Breaking Records," *Oregon Public Broadcasting.*
8 Green, "Air Quality in Portland and Parts of Oregon Is Worse Than in Beijing or Mexico City."

Chapter 2: Out and Back

1 National Wildfire Coordinating Group, "Ten Standard Firefighting Orders."
2 National Wildfire Coordinating Group, "Know Your Fire Shelter." Working on two fires that summer, our crews worked long hours digging fire control lines and pumping water on the flames.
3 History Link, "Mount St. Helens National Volcanic Monument Is Created on August 26."
4 US Department of Agriculture, Forest Service, "Interpretive Site: Layser Cave."
5 "Big Island Ranks #1 Most Diverse County in the U.S.," *KHON2 News*, August 25, 2021.

6 US Fish and Wildlife Service, "Hawai'i: 'Paradise' Also Known as Endangered Species Capital of the World."
7 Oregon Encyclopedia, "Tillamook Burn."

Chapter 3: Volcanoes, Glaciers, and Ancient Lakes

1 "3.5 Magnitude Earthquake Rattles Area South of Portland," KVAL13 online, September 7, 2012.
2 Orr and Orr, *Oregon Geology*, 156–159.
3 Walker and Duncan, *Geologic Map of the Salem 1" by 2" Quadrangle*. Geologic maps like this one display the variety of rocks and sediments exposed within the North Fork watershed and surrounding areas.
4 GeologyIn, "The Colorful Painted Hills in Oregon."
5 White, "Evolution of Calc-Alkaline Magmas at the Quaternary Battle Ax Volcano," 107–122.
6 Walker and Duncan, *Geologic Map of the Salem 1" by 2" Quadrangle*.
7 Sobieszczyk, "Using Turbidity Monitoring and Lidar-Derived Imagery." Excellent descriptions of North Fork landslides along with detailed maps of the watershed. Includes summary of area geology, climate, and precipitation.
8 Steven Sobieszczyk, interview with author, October 22, 2015.

Chapter 4: Since Time before Memory

1 Lewis, "Kalapuyan Eyewitnesses to the Megaflood."
2 Allen, Burns, and Burns, *Cataclysms on the Columbia*, 169–180.
3 Harrelson, "Grand Ronde History 101."
4 Davidson, "Oregon Names," 1.
5 Lewis, *Tribal Histories of the Willamette Valley*, 18.
6 Lewis, "Santiam Forks Band of Molalla."
7 Mackey, *The Kalapuyans*, 11–12.
8 Lewis, "Traditional Sharing of the Cascades Range by Tribes."
9 George, *The Santiam Mining District of the Oregon Cascades: A Cultural Property Inventory and Historical Survey*, 243–246.
10 Juntunen, Dasch, and Rogers, *The World of the Kalapuya*, 30–33.
11 Lewis, "Kalapuyan Tribal History."
12 Lewis, "Santiam Forks Band of Molalla."
13 Lengacher, *History of the North Santiam Canyon*.
14 Confederated Tribes of Grand Ronde, "Native American Plankhouse."
15 Aikens, Connolly, and Jenkins, *Oregon Archaeology*, 295–297.
16 Day, "Kalapuyan Tribal History."
17 Lewis, *Tribal Histories of the Willamette Valley*, 18–20.
18 Juntunen, Dasch, and Rogers, *World of the Kalapuya*, 48–49.
19 Juntunen, Dasch, and Rogers, *World of the Kalapuya*, 30–32.
20 "A Brief History," in Opal Creek Ancient Forest Center, 2016 Catalog, https://www.opalcreek.org/wp-content/uploads/2016/01/Opal-Creek-Catalog-2016-final.pdf.
21 Lewis, *Tribal Histories of the Willamette Valley*, 19.

22 Juntunen, Dasch, and Rogers, *World of the Kalapuya*, 21–22.
23 McCulley Kelly, "Prehistoric Land-Use Patterns in the North Santiam Subbasin," 37–38, 157, 174.
24 Historic Oregon City, "Klamath Trail."

Chapter 5: Trails of Tears

1 Wilkinson, *The People Are Dancing Again*, 57–58.
2 Lewis, *Tribal Histories of the Willamette Valley*, 9–12.
3 Mackey, *The Kalapuyans*, 93–98.
4 Mackey, *The Kalapuyans*, 98–108.
5 Mackey, *The Kalapuyans*, 111–116.
6 "Treaty with the Santiam Band of Molale, 1851." Tribal Treaties Database, Oklahoma State University Libraries.
7 Lewis, "Willamette Valley Treaty (Treaty with the Kalapuya, Etc.)."
8 Lewis, *Tribal Histories of the Willamette Valley*, 83–89.
9 Wilkinson, *The People Are Dancing Again*, 136–148.
10 Wilkinson, *The People Are Dancing Again*, 149–170; Confederated Tribes of Grand Ronde, Trail of Tears.
11 Wilkinson, *The People Are Dancing Again*, 50.
12 Lewis. *Tribal Histories of the Willamette Valley*, 113–130.
13 Stephanie Craig (formerly Stephanie Wood), interview with author, Grand Ronde, Oregon, November 14, 2019. Stephanie is a descendant of the Hudson family, a seventh-generation basket-weaver, artist, and member of the Confederated Tribes of Grand Ronde.
14 US Department of the Interior, Indian Affairs, "Federal Supervision over Western Oregon Indians Terminated."
15 Confederated Tribes of Grand Ronde, "Lands."
16 Wood, "Termination."

Chapter 6: The Gateway

1 Stout, *Lewis Stout Diary—1852*.
2 Stout, "The Mehama Story."
3 Fleetwood, *One Hundred Years in the North Santiam Canyon*.
4 Fleetwood, *One Hundred Years in the North Santiam Canyon*, 3.
5 Stout, "The Mehama Story," 8–9.
6 Iva VanBeek, interview with author, July 9, 2019. Iva grew up in Mehama and was in her late nineties when I met her. She shared her memories from the 1920s, 1930s, and 1940s in Mehama, along the North Fork, and in the surrounding Santiam country.
7 Roberts, *Elkhorn and Mehama*, 55.
8 Roberts, *Elkhorn and Mehama*, 55–56.
9 Stout, "The Mehama Story," 9–11.
10 "Mrs. Smith's Burial," *Oregon Statesman*.
11 Stout, "The Mehama Story," 10–11.

Chapter 7: Seeking Gold

1 "Diary of a Miner on the Santiam River, Oregon, 1864," Oregon Historical Society.
2 George, *Santiam Mining District of the Oregon Cascades: A Cultural Property Inventory and Historical Survey*, 78.
3 "The Capital Mine," *Weekly Oregon Statesman.*
4 George, *Santiam Mining District of the Oregon Cascades: A Cultural Property Inventory and Historical Survey*, 37–39.
5 George, *Santiam Mining District of the Oregon Cascades: A Cultural Property Inventory and Historical Survey*, 53–54.
6 Roberts, *Elkhorn and Mehama*, 55, 21–22.
7 Fleetwood, *One Hundred Years in the North Santiam Canyon*, 5–6.
8 Grafe, *Gates of the North Santiam*, 7.
9 George Atiyeh, interview with author, December 17, 2013. I spoke with George numerous times through the years about the mines and canyon history.
10 George Atiyeh, interview with author, December 17, 2013.
11 Lengacher, *History of the North Santiam Canyon*; Cindi Budlong, "James Church and the Storm of 1884."

Chapter 8: Newcomers

1 Mason, "Pioneers on the Santiam."
2 Lau, *A History of the North Santiam River Crossings*, 8.
3 "Covered Bridges in Marion County," *Marion County History*, 3–5.
4 Norma Pennington, interview with author, February 6, 2017.
5 Bill Hueller, interview with author, February 28, 2018.
6 Grafe, *Gates of the North Santiam.*
7 Little North Santiam Watershed Analysis, Appendix F, Bureau of Land Management, https://www.fs.usda.gov/sites/nfs/files/r06/willamette/publication/Little_North_Santiam_combined_compressed.pdf.
8 Randall, *Elkhorn: A Lifetime of Memories*, 7–9; Grafe, *Gates of the North Santiam*, 10.

Chapter 9: Fire, Logging, and Conservation

1 Craig V. Randall, interview with author, December 30, 2019. Craig V. Randall has known the North Fork for more than seventy years. His father, Craig Z. Randall, wrote the self-published book titled *A Lifetime of Memories.*
2 Rakestraw and Rakestraw, *History of the Willamette National Forest.*
3 "Diary of Chet Kubin, February 24, 1928–March 25, 1930," *Santiam Historical Society*, 152–160. The Santiam Historical Society is based in Stayton, Oregon (not to be confused with the North Santiam Historical Society in Mill City).
4 Rakestraw and Rakestraw, *History of the Willamette National Forest*, 197.
5 "Spreading Fire Forces Partial Evacuation of North Santiam Areas," Albany *Democrat-Herald.*

6 Phyllis Fencl and Alice Bickett, interview with author, December 7, 2021. Phyllis and Alice lived on their parent's ranch in Elkhorn Valley at the time of the Sardine Creek Fire. Their ranch is described more in chapter 12.
7 Pinchot Institute for Conservation Studies, "The Lands Nobody Wanted."
8 Snead, *Judge John B. Waldo*, 77–78.
9 Snead, *Judge John B. Waldo*, 79–82.
10 Puter and Stevens, *Looters of the Public Domain.*
11 Parkinson, "Silverton's Skid Shacks."
12 Fleetwood, *One Hundred Years in the North Santiam Canyon*, 15.
13 Posekany, *Some History of Frank Lumber Company.*
14 Dennis Frank, interview with author, April 12, 2017. Dennis Frank is the president of Frank Lumber Company in Mill City, Oregon, and the son of Mandy Frank.
15 Robert (Bob) Freres, interview with author, November 3, 2017. Robert Freres became president of Freres Lumber Company in Lyons, Oregon, in 1968. He was the son of Ted Freres and passed away in 2019.
16 Wentz, *Bringing Out the Big Ones*, 11, 15–17, and 35.
17 Dale Kirsch, interview with author, March 14, 2016.
18 Dale Kirsch, Terry Gookin and Al Ketchum, interviews with author, March 8, 2017.
19 Gordon Kirsch, interview with author, June 20, 2018.

Chapter 10: Tree Army Boys and Cloud Girls

1 Cara Kelly, interview with author, August 7, 2015.
2 Alan Maul, interview with author, November 13, 2018.
3 "Up and Coming," *Civilian Conservation Corps Santiam Canyon Newsletter*, 32.
4 "Forest Men Arrive," *Daily Capital Journal.*
5 Cara Kelly, interview with author, August 7, 2015.
6 Alan Maul, interview with author, November 13, 2018; "Forest Lookouts—Marion County"; Kresek, *Fire Lookouts of the Northwest*, 33–35. Besides the lookouts on Henline and Battle Ax, other lookouts built by the CCCs surrounding the North Fork included lookout cabins on House Mountain, Lookout Mountain, Whetstone Mountain, and Rocky Top.
7 Dorothy G. Middleton (Crawford), Battle Ax Mountain Lookout Station, 1943 (unpublished journal), Detroit Ranger Station, Willamette National Forest.
8 Gachman, "The History of Lady Lookouts."
9 Nelson, *History of Silver Falls*, 94–104.

Chapter 11: A Modern-Day Parable

1 Iva VanBeek, interviews with author, July 9 and September 24, 2019. Iva grew up in Mehama and was in her late nineties when I met her. She shared her memories from the 1920s, 1930s and 1940s in Mehama, along the North Fork and in the surrounding Santiam country.

Chapter 12: Primitive Beauty

1 Roberts, *Elkhorn and Mehama*, 55, 10–12.
2 Todd Mobley, interview with author, July 25, 2017. Todd and his family lived many years along the North Fork near Taylor's Grove, and he carries a wide knowledge of area history.
3 McKay, *An Editor for Oregon*, 261.
4 Floyd J. McKay, interview, August 3, 2016.
5 Todd Mobley, interview with author, July 25, 2017.
6 Floyd J. McKay, interview, August 3, 2016.
7 McKay, *An Editor for Oregon*, 264.
8 McKay, *An Editor for Oregon*, 275; Jim Fisher, *Honoring a Century of Service*, 36–37.
9 Randall, *Elkhorn: A Lifetime of Memories*, 34–37.
10 Randall, *Elkhorn: A Lifetime of Memories*, 35.
11 Brad Green, interview with author, August 11, 2018. Brad is a descendent of one of the original Elkhorn Corporation members. He and his family have shared their Elkhorn stories with me through the years.
12 Roberts, *Elkhorn and Mehama*, 62–63.
13 "Cranberry House," *Mill City Enterprise.*

Chapter 13: Things That Came . . .

1 Roberts, *Ten Years of Mehama*, 62–63.
2 Roberts, *Ten Years of Mehama*, 35–36.
3 Liz Cutler, interview with author, March 23, 2016. Liz Cutler's father, Don Cutler, developed the original nine-hole golf course. She recalled his work creating this course in Elkhorn Valley.
4 Lyman, "Reminiscences of Louis Labonte."
5 Roberts, *Elkhorn and Mehama*, 18.
6 "Recovering Oregon's Most Imperiled Salmon and Steelhead," Native Fish Society, accessed July 15, 2025, https://nativefishsociety.org/campaigns/rewild-the-willamette.
7 "Elkhorn Falls Fishway," *Statesman Journal.*
8 National Oceanic and Atmospheric Administration Fisheries, "Lack of Passage Drives Continued Decline of Upper Willamette Chinook Salmon and Steelhead."
9 Johnston, "Grand Ronde Gathers to Celebrate Salmon."
10 Willamette Basin Task Force, "Willamette Basin Comprehensive Study."
11 "Elkhorn Developer Making the Rounds," *Stayton Mail.*
12 The Bornite Project, Oregon Department of Geology, 1992, https://www.oregon.gov/dogami/milo/archive/MiningDistricts/MarionCounty/NorthSantiamDistrict/BorniteProject/BorniteProjectReports.pdf.

Chapter 14: Battle for Opal Creek

1 George Atiyeh, interview with author, December 17, 2013.
2 The Wilderness Society, "The Wilderness Act."

3 Seideman, *Showdown at Opal Creek.*
4 Tom Atiyeh, interview with author, May 1, 2019.
5 The Wilderness Society, "The Roadless Rule: A Tenth Anniversary Assessment."
6 Urness, "In the 1970s, Salem Residents Fought for the 'Hidden Wilderness.'"
7 Anthony J. George, interview with author, April 17, 2021; John Brandt, interview with the author, May 2, 2025.
8 Central Cascades Conservation Council, *A Hiker's Guide to Oregon's Hidden Wilderness.*
9 Kerr, "Oregon Wilderness by the Numbers."
10 Urness, "Timeline of Events: The Fight for Opal Creek."
11 George, *Santiam Mining District of the Oregon Cascades: A Cultural Property Inventory and Historical Survey.*
12 Anthony J. George, interview with author, April 17, 2021.
13 Olson, "Photographer Helped Save Opal Creek."
14 Postrel, "Foes Log Feelings on Cascade Park."
15 OpenLibrary, "Opal Creek Forest Preserve Act."
16 Urness, "How Mark Hatfield, Unlikely Hero, Saved Opal Creek."
17 Opal Creek Ancient Forest Center, "Opal Creek Ancient Forest Center History."
18 Tom Atiyeh, interview with author, May 1, 2019.
19 US Department of Agriculture, Forest Service, "Establishment of the Opal Creek Wilderness and Opal Creek Scenic Recreation Area."

Chapter 15: Beachie Creek Fire, 2020

1 John Spencer, interview with author, March 8, 2022.
2 Eric Perkins, interview with author, January 20, 2022.
3 Don Everingham, interview with author, February 4, 2022.
4 Ken Cartwright, interview with author, May 4, 2024.
5 US Department of Agriculture, Forest Service, "2020 Beachie Creek Fire Storymap—Chapter 3." Chapter 3 of this document describes the 2020 Labor Day wind event. Also see US Department of Agriculture, Forest Service, "Beachie Creek Fire" (overview).
6 "'Reluctant Heroes' Honored as Mill City Remembers Beachie Creek Fire Anniversary," *Salem Reporter.*
7 Don Myron, interview with author, July 31, 2021.
8 Scott Torgeson, interview with author, October 16, 2023.
9 John Spencer, interview with author, March 8, 2022.
10 Federal Emergency Management Agency, "Beachie Creek Fire—Erosion Threat Assessment/Reduction Team (ETART) Summary Report."
11 Oregon Department of Forestry, "2020 Labor Day Fires: Post-Fire Challenges with Invasive Plants."
12 Paul, "Timber Company Begins Salvage after Wildfire."
13 "After Record Fire Season, Oregon Researchers Say Wildfires Will Only Get Worse," *KGW8+: Wildfire.*

Chapter 16: Beautiful Stream

1 Lynn, "Santiam Canyon Strong Quilts Comfort Families Three Months after Wildfires," *Statesman Journal.*

2 "Merkley Announces $15 Million for the Opal Creek Promise," Jeff Merkley Senator for Oregon website.

Bibliography

"After Record Fire Season, Oregon Researchers Say Wildfires Will Only Get Worse." By Keely Chalmers. *KGW8+: Wildfire*. September 21, 2021. https://www.kgw.com/article/news/local/wildfire/experts-on-wildfires-preparation/283-cf27e582-91a6-44c9-b413-150aab3e77b8.

Aikens, Melvin C., Thomas J. Connolly, and Dennis L. Jenkins. *Oregon Archaeology*. Oregon State University Press, 2011.

Allen, J. Eliot, Marjorie Burns, and Scott Burns. *Cataclysms on the Columbia*. Ooligan Press, 2009.

"Big Island Ranks #1 Most Diverse County in the U.S." By Mariya Parkhomchuk. *KHON2 News*. August 25, 2021. https://www.khon2.com/local-news/big-island-ranks-1-most-diverse-county-in-us.

Budlong, Cindi. "James Church and the Storm of 1884." *North Santiam Historical Society Fall Newsletter*, 2025.

"The Capital Mine." Weekly *Oregon Statesman*, August 10, 1888. https://www.newspapers.com/image/81247034/?match=1&terms=The%20Capital%20Mine.

Central Cascades Conservation Council. *A Hiker's Guide to Oregon's Hidden Wilderness*. Central Cascades Conservation Council, 1976.

Confederated Tribes of Grand Ronde. "Native American Plankhouse." https://www.grandronde.org/media/ojwbh2z2/6mthplankhouse-read-aloud.pdf.

Confederated Tribes of Grand Ronde. "Lands." Accessed July 14, 2025. https://www.grandronde.org/government/lands.

Confederated Tribes of Grand Ronde. "Trail of Tears." Accessed August 25, 2025. https://www.grandronde.org/culture-history/trail-of-tears/.

"Covered Bridges in Marion County." *Marion County History*. Vol. 2. Marion County Historical Society, Salem, OR, 1956. Located at Willamette Heritage Center, Salem, OR.

"Cranberry House." *Mill City Enterprise*, March 27, 1958. Located at Canyon Life Museum, Mill City, OR.

Davidson, A. F. "Oregon Names." *Willamette Farmer Newspaper*, January 1, 1875. https://oregonnews.uoregon.edu/lccn/sn85042522/1875-01-01/ed-1/seq-1/.

Day, Don. "Kalapuyan Tribal History." Presentation at interagency tour, Sweet Home, OR, June 2, 2017.

"Diary of Chet Kubin, February 24, 1928–March 25, 1930." Santiam Historical Society, Stayton, OR.

"Diary of a Miner on the Santiam River, Oregon, 1864." Oregon Historical Society, Portland, OR.

"Elkhorn Developer Making the Rounds." *Stayton Mail,* March 28, 2007.

"Elkhorn Falls Fishway." *Statesman Journal,* February 12, 1962.

Federal Emergency Management Agency. "Beachie Creek Fire—Erosion Threat Assessment/Reduction Team (ETART) Summary Report." December 2020. https://digitalcollections.library.oregon.gov/nodes/view/276639.

Fisher, Jim. *Honoring a Century of Service: The Centennial History of the Oregon Board of Forestry and the Oregon Department of Forestry 1911–2011.* Oregon Department of Forestry. April 2011. Located at Forest History Center and Museum, Salem, OR.

Fleetwood, Evangeline. *One Hundred Years in the North Santiam Canyon.* c. 1986. North Santiam Historical Society, Mill City, OR.

"Forest Lookouts—Marion County." Accessed August 25, 2025. https://oregon-lookouts.weebly.com.

"Forest Men Arrive." *Daily Capital Journal,* May 31, 1933. https://www.newspapers.com/image/94833757/?match=1&terms=forest%20men%20arrive.

Gachman, Dina. "The History of Lady Lookouts." *Smithsonian* (online). March 29, 2021. https://www.smithsonianmag.com/history/female-fire-lookouts-have-been-sving-wilderness-over-century-180977352._

GeologyIn. "The Colorful Painted Hills in Oregon." Accessed July 14, 2025. https://www.geologyin.com/2014/05/these-colorful-hills-in-oregon-create.html.

George, Anthony J. *The Santiam Mining District of the Oregon Cascades: A Cultural Property Inventory and Historical Survey.* Solo Press, 1985.

Grafe, Willis. *Gates of the North Santiam.* Self-published, 1989. Located at Canyon Life Museum, Mill City, OR.

Green, Aimee. "Air Quality in Portland and Parts of Oregon Worse Than Beijing or Mexico City, due to Wildfire Smoke." *Oregonian,* September 10, 2020._https://www.oregonlive.com/news/2020/09/air-quality-in-portland-is-worse-than-in-beijing-mumbai-or-mexico-city-due-to-wildfire-smoke.

Hansen, Heather. *Prophets and Moguls, Rangers, and Rogues, Bison, and Bears—100 Years of the National Park Service.* Mountaineers Books, 2015.

Harrelson, David. "Grand Ronde History 101." Presentation at Culture and History Summit, Grand Ronde, OR, October 26, 2016.

Hartmans, Donna Marie. "Historic Lookout Stations on the Willamette National Forest: Management Plans for Preservation." Master's thesis, University of Oregon, 1991.

Historic Oregon City. "Klamath Trail." By Bethany Nemec. Historic Oregon City. April 3, 2019. https://historicoregoncity.org/2019/04/03/klamath-trail.

History Link. "Mount St. Helens National Volcanic Monument Is Created on August 26." Accessed April 17, 2024. https://www.historylink.org.

Johnston, Mariah. "Grand Ronde Gathers to Celebrate Salmon, New Conservation Area on North Santiam." *Statesman Journal*, June 10, 2025.

Juntunen, Judy Rycraft, May D. Dasch, and Ann Bennett Rogers. *The World of the Kalapuya: A Native People of Western Oregon*. Benton County Historical Society and Museum, 2005.

Kerr, Andy. *Oregon Wild: Endangered Forest Wilderness*. Oregon Natural Resources Council, 2004.

Kerr, Andy. "Oregon Wilderness by the Numbers: Versus Adjacent States Congressional Delegation Rankings, and Total Potential Wilderness." *Public Lands* (blog), May 24, 2019. https://www.andykerr.net/kerr-public-lands-blog/2019/5/22/oregon-wilderness-by-the-numbers-versus-adjacent-states-congressional-delegation-rankings-and-total-potential-wilderness.

Kresek, Ray. *Fire Lookouts of the Northwest*. Ye Galleon Press, 1998.

Lau, Ernst. *A History of the North Santiam River Crossings*. Santiam Heritage Foundation, 2001.

Lengacher, John. *History of the North Santiam Canyon*. Unpublished manuscript. Circa 1994. Canyon Life Museum, Mill City, OR.

Lewis, David G. "Kalapuyan Eyewitnesses to the Megaflood in the Willamette Valley." *Quartux Journal* (blog), April 8, 2017. https://ndnhistoryresearch.com/2017/04/08/kalapuyan-eyewitnesses-to-the-megaflood-in-the-willamette-valley/comment-page-1.

Lewis, David G. "Santiam Forks Band of Molalla." *Quartux Journal* (blog), October 17, 2021. https://ndnhistoryresearch.com/molalla-ethnohistory.

Lewis, David G. "Traditional Sharing of the Cascades Range by Tribes." *Quartux Journal* (blog), November 12, 2018. https://ndnhistoryresearch.com/2018/11/12/traditional-sharing-of-the-cascades-range-by-tribes.

Lewis, David G. *Tribal Histories of the Willamette Valley*. Ooligan Press, 2023.

Lewis, David G. "Willamette Valley Treaty (Treaty with the Kalapuya, Etc.) Signed January 22, Ratified March 3, 1855." *Quartux Journal* (blog), January 16, 2018. https://nndnhistoryresearch.com/2018/01/16/the-willamette-valley-treaty-treaty-with-the-kalapuya-etc-signed-january-22-ratified-march-3-1855.

Liittschwager, David and Susan Middleton. *Remains of a Rainbow: Rare Plants and Animals of Hawai'i*. National Geographic Society, 2001.

Lyman, H. S. "Reminiscences of Louis Labonte." *Oregon History Quarterly* 1, no. 1 (1900). https://en.wikisource.org/wiki/Oregon_Historical_Quarterly/Volume_1/Reminiscences_of_Louis_Labonte.

Lynn, Capi. "Santiam Canyon Strong' Quilts Comfort Families Three Months after Wildfires." *Statesman Journal*, December 5, 2020. https://www.statesmanjournal.com/story/news/2020/12/05/santiam-canyon-beachie-creek-oregon-wildfire-victim-fquilts-homes/3833655001/.

Mackey, Harold. *The Kalapuyans: A Sourcebook on the Indians of the Willamette Valley*. 2nd ed. Mission Mill Museum Association (now Willamette Heritage Center), Salem OR, 2004.

Mason, Sue. "Pioneers on the Santiam." Unknown newspaper and publication date (clipping contained in a scrapbook of Norma Pennington). Located at Canyon Life Museum, Mill City, OR.

McCulley Kelly, Cara. "Prehistoric Land-Use Patterns in the North Santiam Subbasin on the Western Slopes of the Oregon Cascade Range." Master's thesis, Oregon State University, 2001.

McKay, Floyd J. *An Editor for Oregon: Charles A. Sprague and the Politics of Change*. Oregon State University Press, 1998.

"Merkley Announces $15 Million for the Opal Creek Promise." Jeff Merkley Senator for Oregon website. September 21, 2023. https://merkley.senate.gov/merkley-announces-15-million-for-the-opal-creek-promise.

"Mrs. Smith's Burial." *Oregon Statesman*, April 11, 1895. https://www.newspapers.com/image/198555041/?match=1&terms=mrs%20smith%20burial.

National Oceanic and Atmospheric Administration Fisheries. "Lack of Passage Drives Continued Decline of Upper Willamette Chinook Salmon and Steelhead." July 9, 2024. https://www.fisheries.noaa.gov/feature-story/lack-passage-drives-continued-decline-upper-willamette-chinook-salmon-and-steelhead.

National Weather Service. "Beachie Creek Fire, Northwest Oregon." December 28, 2020. https://storymaps.arcgis.com/stories/b9d08274bca54e2d9f87b7c040b6f02b.

National Wildfire Coordinating Group. "Know Your Fire Shelter." Accessed July 14, 2025. https://www.nwcg.gov/publications/pms411/know-your-fire-shelter.

National Wildfire Coordinating Group. "Ten Standard Firefighting Orders." Accessed July 14, 2025. https://www.nwcg.gov/6mfs/operational-engagement/10-standard-firefighting-orders.

Native Fish Society. "Recovering Oregon's Most Imperiled Salmon and Steelhead." Accessed July 15, 2025. https://nativefishsociety.org/campaigns/rewild-the-willamette.

Nelson, Andrew K. *The History of Silver Falls*. Friends of Silver Falls State Park, 2013.

Olson, Larry N. "Photographer Helped Save Opal Creek." *Larry N. Olson Photographer* (blog). July 16, 2016. https://larrynolson.com/blog/photographer-helped-save-opal-creek/.

Opal Creek Ancient Forest Center. "Opal Creek Ancient Forest Center History." Accessed July 16, 2025. https://opalcreek.org/about/.

OpenLibrary. "Opal Creek Forest Preserve Act." Internet Archive, December 17, 2025. https://openlibrary.org/books/OL893001M/Opal_Creek_Forest_Preserve_Act.

Oregon Department of Forestry. "2020 Labor Day Fires: Post-Fire Challenges with Invasive Plants." Forest Facts, May 2022. https://www.oregon.gov/odf/Documents/forestbenefits/fact-sheet-labor-day-fire-weeds.pdf.

Oregon Encyclopedia. "Tillamook Burn." Accessed July 14, 2025. https://www.oregonencyclopedia.org/articles/tillamook_burn.

"Oregon's Air Is So Hazardous It's Breaking Records." *Oregon Public Broadcasting*, September 15, 2020. https://www.opb.org/article/2020/09/15/oregons-air-is-so-hazardous-its-breaking-records.

Orr, Elizabeth L., and William N. Orr. *Oregon Geology.* Oregon State University Press, 2012.

Parkinson, Fred A. "Silverton's Skid Shacks." *Silverton Country Historical Society Newsletter* 13, no, 3 (April 2015). https://www.silvertonmuseum.org/newsletters/schs_nl_201504.pdf.

Paul, Alex. "Timber Company Begins Salvage after Wildfire." Albany *Democrat-Herald*, October 30, 2020. https://oregonnews.uoregon.edu/lccn/sn83008376/2020-10-31/ed-1/seq-17.pdf.

Pinchot Institute for Conservation Studies. "The Lands Nobody Wanted: The Legacy of the Eastern National Forests." https://foresthistory.org/wp-content/uploads/2017/01/LandsNobodyWanted_Shands.pdf.

Posekany, Dick. *Some History of Frank Lumber Company*. Mt. Angel Publishing, 2010.

Postrel, Dan. "Foes Log Feelings on Cascades Park." *Statesman Journal*, February 22, 1989. https://www.newspapers.com/image/200355082/?match=1&terms=Foes%20Log%20Feelings%20on%20Cascades%20Park.

Puter, S. A. D., and Horace Stevens. *Looters of the Public Domain.* Portland Printing House, 1908.

Quiring, James P. *Mount St. Helens: The Continuing Story*. KC Publications, 1991.

Rakestraw, Lawrence, and Mary Rakestraw. *History of the Willamette National Forest*. US Department of Agriculture, Forest Service. 1991. https://foresthistory.org/wp-content/uploads/2017/01/HISTORY-OF-THE-WILLAMETTE-NATIONAL-FOREST.pdf.

Randall, Craig Z. *Elkhorn: A Lifetime of Memories.* Self-published, 2003.

Reinhardt, Bob H. *Struggle on the North Santiam: Power and Community on the Margins of the American West.* Oregon State University Press, 2020.

"'Reluctant Heroes' Honored as Mill City Remembers Beachie Creek Fire Anniversary." *Salem Reporter*, September 7, 2021. https://www.salemreporter.com/2021/09/07/reluctant-heroes-honored-as-mill-city-remembers-beachie-creek-fire-anniversary.

Roberts, Jean. *Elkhorn and Mehama: True Stories of Oregonians of the North Santiam*. Mehama Press, c. 1956. Located at Canyon Life Museum, Mill City, OR.

Roberts, Jean. *Ten Years of Mehama: True Stories of Oregonians of the North Santiam.* Mehama Press, c. 1956. Located at Canyon Life Museum, Mill City, OR.

Schweitzer, Sophia V. *Big Island Journey: An Illustrated Narrative of the Island of Hawai'i*. Mutual Publishing, 2009.

Seideman, David. *Showdown at Opal Creek: The Battle for America's Last Wilderness*. Carroll & Graf, 1993.

Snead, Bobbie. *Judge John B. Waldo: Oregon's John Muir*. Maverick Publications, 2006.

Sobieszczyk, Steven. "Using Turbidity Monitoring and Lidar-Derived Imagery to Investigate Sources of Suspended Sediment in the Little North Santiam River Basin, Oregon." PhD diss., Portland State University, 2010. https://pdxscholar.library.pdx.edu/open_access_etds/176/.

"Spreading Fire Forces Partial Evacuation of North Santiam Areas." Albany *Democrat-Herald*, September 21, 1951. https://www.newspapers.com/article/albany-democrat-herald-sardine-creek-fir/13012868.

Stout, Lewis. *Lewis Stout Diary—1852*. Oregon Historical Society Research Library. https://researchworks.oclc.org/archivegrid/collection/data/31784078.

Stout, Ray L. "The Mehama Story." *Marion County History* 10 (1969–71). Located at Willamette Heritage Center, Salem, OR.

"3.5 Magnitude Earthquake Rattles Area South of Portland." KVAL13 online, September 7, 2012. https://kval.com/news/local/35-magnitude-earthquake-rattles-area-south-of-portland.

"Treaty with the Santiam Band of Molale, 1851." Tribal Treaties Database, Oklahoma State University Libraries. https://treaties.okstate.edu/treaties/treaty-with-the-santiam-band-of-molale-1851-22525.

"Up and Coming." *Civilian Conservation Corps Santiam Canyon* newsletter, September 1933. Forest History Center, Salem, OR.

Urness, Zach. "How Mark Hatfield, Unlikely Hero, Saved Opal Creek." *Statesman Journal*, September 24, 2016. https://www.statesmanjournal.com/story/news/2016/09/24/mark-hatfield-opal-creek-oregon-hiking/90417548.

Urness, Zach. "In the 1970s, Salem Residents Fought for the 'Hidden Wilderness.'" *Statesman Journal*, September 24, 2016. https://www.statesmanjournal.com/story/news/2016/09/24/1970's-salem-residents-fought-hidden-wilderness/90383538.

Urness, Zach. "Oregon Wildfires: How the Tiny Beachie Creek Fire Blew Up and Ravaged the Santiam Canyon." *Statesman Journal*, September 12, 2020. https://www.statesmanjournal.com/story/news/2020/09/12/beachie-creek-fire-growth-oregon-santiam-canyon/3474149001.

Urness, Zach. "Timeline of Events: The Fight for Opal Creek." *Statesman Journal*, September 24, 2016. https://www.statesmanjournal.com/story/news/2016/09/24/timeline-events-fight-opal-creek/90757086/.

US Department of Agriculture, Forest Service. "Bornite Underground Copper Mine Project: Environmental Impact Statement (1993)." https://searchworks.stanford.edu/view/2895406.

US Department of Agriculture, Forest Service. "Establishment of the Opal Creek Wilderness and Opal Creek Scenic Recreation Area, Willamette National Forest, Marion County, Oregon." *Federal Register* 63, no 223. November 19, 1998. https://www.govinfo.gov/content/pkg/FR-1998-11-19/pdf/98-30912.pdf.

US Department of Agriculture, Forest Service. "Highlights in the History of Forest Conservation." AIB-83. March 1976. https://archive.org/details/CAT87210826/page/n1/mode/2up.

US Department of Agriculture, Forest Service. "Interpretive Site: Layser Cave." Accessed July 14, 2025. https://www.fs.usda.gov/r06/giffordpinchot/recreation/interpretive-site-layser-cave.

US Department of Agriculture, Forest Service. "Beachie Creek Fire" (overview). Accessed March 10, 2026. https://www.fs.usda.gov/r06/willamette/fire/info/beachie-creek-fire.

US Department of Agriculture, Forest Service. "2020 Beachie Creek Fire Storymap." All chapters archived and available by request from the Willamette National Forest Supervisors Office in Springfield, OR.

US Department of the Interior, Indian Affairs. "Federal Supervision over Western Oregon Indians Terminated." August 14, 1956. https://www.bia.gov/as-ia/opa/online-press-release/federal-supervision-over-western-oregon-indians-terminated.

US Fish and Wildlife Service. "Hawai'i: 'Paradise' Also Known as Endangered Species Capital of the World." May 18, 2016. https://www.fws.gov/story/2016-05/hawaii-paradise-also-known-endangered-species-capital-world.

Walker, George W., and Robert A. Duncan, *Geologic Map of the Salem 1" by 2" Quadrangle, Western Oregon.* US Geological Survey, 1989. https://doi.org/10.3133/i1893.

Wentz, Walt. *Bringing Out the Big Ones: Log Trucking in Oregon 1912–1983.* Oregon Forest Products Association, 1985.

White, Craig M. "Evolution of Calc-Alkaline Magmas at the Quaternary Battle Ax Volcano, Western Cascade Range, Oregon." *Journal of Volcanology and Geothermal Research* 52, no. 1/3 (1992). https://www.sciencedirect.com/science/article/abs/pii/037702739290135Z.

The Wilderness Society. "The Roadless Rule: A Tenth Anniversary Assessment." By Michael Anderson. https://www.wilderness.org/sites/default/files/media/file/Roadless-Rule-paper-10th-anniversary.pdf.

The Wilderness Society. "The Wilderness Act." Accessed July 16, 2025. https://www.wilderness.org/articles/article/wilderness-act/.

Wilkinson, Charles. *The People Are Dancing Again: The History of the Siletz Tribe of Western Oregon.* University of Washington Press, 2010.

Willamette Basin Task Force. "Willamette Basin Comprehensive Study: Water and Related Land Resources: Appendix M—Plan Formulation." Pacific Northwest River Basins Commission, 1969. https://openlibrary.org/books/OL5021065M/

Willamette_Basin_comprehensive_study_of_water_and_related_land_resources.

Wood, Stephanie. "Termination." *Honoring Tribal Legacies* (blog). University of Oregon. Accessed August 21, 2025. https://blogs.uoregon.edu/honoringtriballegacies/primary-sources/termination.

Index

Page numbers in italics indicate images.

www.ingramcontent.com/pod-product-compliance
Lightning Source LLC
LaVergne TN
LVHW011029131026
850117LV00038B/443